THE COLONEL'S NOTEBOOK

A collection of articles and anecdotes from a
soldier of the
British Raj in India

By

**Colonel James William Caldwell
Hutchinson**

Aided and Abetted

By

Henry Butterfield

Text © HENRY BUTTERFIELD 2017

Cover design © HENRY BUTTERFIELD 2017

Photographs © HENRY BUTTERFIELD 2017

Published by The Cherry Tree Press

First Edition

Also, available as a Kindle eBook

The author asserts his moral right under the copyright, Designs, and Patents Act 1988 to be identified as the author of this work.

All rights reserved. No part of this publication may be reproduced, stored in a retrieval system, or transmitted, in any form or by any means without the prior consent of the author, nor be otherwise circulated in any form of binding or cover other than that in which it is published and without a similar condition being imposed on the subsequent purchaser.

The Dedication

I would like to give a special thank you to Graham and Sophie Leach. Sadly, Sophie is no longer with us, but she was instrumental in rescuing several artefacts from the flames of the bonfire, especially photographs and other pictures. And of course, I must thank Graham, for being the faithful custodian of all this valuable folk history.

I would also like to thank all those kind people who allow their photos and pictures to be used free of charge through the Creative Commons. More detailed thanks are at the rear of the book. If I have breached anyone's copyright, please contact me and the offending picture will be removed immediately.

Finally, a great many thanks to my long-suffering wife, Evelyn. For all the lonely hours, she spends while her husband sits with pen in hand or is tapping away at a computer keyboard in the study or down the writing shed, once again thank you for your patience. Evelyn, I love you; you're one in a million.

Books by the same author:

❀ **Up the Garden Path** ❀

A short memoir on opening a garden for the National Gardens Scheme while being filmed for television. Available on Amazon.co.uk and Amazon.com and all other countries being served by Amazon. Also, available as a Kindle eBook.

❀ **Retrospective Voices** ❀

My contributions to this First World War anthology (compiled by old Open University creative writing students) are two short stories and a poem. It is available as a Kindle eBook on Amazon.co.uk and Amazon.com and all other countries being served by Amazon.

TABLE OF CONTENTS.

Introduction.

Part 1 – Articles and Observations Made on Active Service.

1) Camp of Exercise – Delhi 1885-86. (Young Lieutenant.)
2) Delhi, 1868 and Afterthought. (Young Lieutenant.)
3) A Pathan Joke, 1890. (Captain.)
4) Bannu to Hunza. 1892. (Captain.)
5) Saraghari, 1897. (Captain.)
6) A Burglary That Failed. 1905-1907. (Lieutenant Colonel.)

Part 2 – Articles and Observations Made After Retirement.

7) Two Epitaphs and Some Incidents.
8) Tales of a Rambler or Eccentricities.
9) Extracts from the Leaves of a Viceroy's Notebook.
10) Native Petition.
11) The History of Kate and Reversals.

Part 3 – His Final Word and His Reader's Comments.

13) Bathos.
14) Criticisms – 1
15) Criticisms – 2

A Short glossary.

A Short Bibliography of Interesting Publications about this period.

INTRODUCTION

Lieutenant Colonel Hutchinson's daughter Sheila died in 1999 aged 93. Within the fields of art and calligraphy she was one of Bideford's well known and important characters. Many examples of her work are on display in the town's Burton Art Gallery and Museum, of which she was a staunch supporter and committee member. Sheila inherited this love of the arts through her father, Colonel James William Caldwell Hutchinson, who besides being an accomplished amateur painter also penned many pieces of writing, of which this journal contains several. This book is a collection of thoughts, anecdotes, and "would be" articles for The Amateur Magazine, where he recalls his adventures in India during the height of the British Empire.

Much has been written about the broad sweep of the British Raj, but this is an intimate insight into the reality for individuals. Some of these realities included; difficulties in getting from place to place, the constant presence of sudden death from attack or disease, and characters with large personalities and strange idiosyncrasies. These articles are tales of real people, in real situations. And these were observed first hand by someone who was there, well over 100 years ago.

This is of course a military tale, and Lieutenant Colonel Hutchinson writes as a Victorian military man, and an officer at that. He is by turn pompous, condescending, snobbish, and opinionated.

Occasionally though, the sentimental and caring side of his character slips from beneath the stiff upper lip; a lip that is heavily disguised by his wonderful, bushy, handlebar moustache. But, although he appears to be 'superior,' the Colonel still has a sense of humour as is revealed in the articles "Tales of a Rambler" and "Native Petition." He is by no means a politically correct person. He is into shooting for sport, and taking animal trophies, and has a very strong empirical streak. He is a true son of Victorian and Edwardian Britain.

In his book, "The Road to Wigan Pier" George Orwell managed to sum up the background of the Colonel, and others of the 'upper-middle class.' He highlighted the strange condition of their existence. They were in effect, in no-man's land. They owned no land, and were not of the industrial or trading type. Rather, they looked to the military, the church, and the professions for their history and traditions. They whole-heartedly felt that although they were not rich, they should be landowners with a touch of the aristocracy. As Orwell brings out, in theory, they knew how to deal with servants, but, in truth, they could only afford one or two at most. They knew how to dress smartly and elegantly, and how to order a meal. But again, the true face of reality was that they could not afford clothes from a quality tailor, or to eat at a superior restaurant. They knew how to shoot and ride, but had no horses and no land on which to hunt and shoot. This is what attracted the likes of them to India, and later, Africa. It was certainly not the place to get rich, but they could at least play at being aristocratic. In India, they would find cheap horses, untold free shooting, and a bottomless well of native servants. As you read the "Colonel's Notebook," you will see this mentality and outlook become evident.

All things must end, and sad circumstances caused the Colonel to leave his beloved India. The date of the event is unknown but before she died his daughter recalled that he managed to pick up an infection. This grew progressively worse and eventually became a long-term health problem. It finally became obvious that the Indian climate was not going to aid his recovery so he was invalided out of the army and sent home. Sheila went on to comment that his enforced retirement and subsequent return to England upset him greatly. It was sometime later that the Colonel began his adventures in the art of biographical writing.

It is remarkable to think though, that this man's unique memoirs could have been lost forever. I discovered the little black notebook and its historic contents in a box of general bric-a-brac that had been put into a general auction after the Hutchinson's house had been cleared. This was just as Sheila prepared to enter a nursing home and see out her final days.

How this notebook escaped a tragic fate borders on a miracle, any amount of valuable "folk" history was destroyed during the house clearance. Unfortunately, I wasn't there when the sorry deed occurred so I was unable to save anything. Sophie Leach, Sheila's general home help, said that the house was like Tutankhamen's tomb, "full of wonderful things." It took days to clear the house. But, in no way was it a simple case of removing the furniture and effects. Over the years, the family had thrown nothing away. As time went by, in the same rooms, the family threw one layer of papers and possessions on top of another so that in time the papers, clothes, and other items, became in effect, stratified. In truth, the whole operation should have been treated like an archaeological dig, slowly sifting out things of interest and importance, layer by layer. Unfortunately, it seems that time did not allow that luxury and inevitably so much of worth, not financial worth, but historical worth, was consigned to Gehenna. It went up in the flames of destruction from the bonfire that burned in the garden of Tower House for many days.

This last little survivor of that conflagration is what follows. Written by the Colonel in his own hand. His eccentric punctuation has been left in, as has his inconsistent use of capital letters. He uses old fashioned, long, Victorian style sentences, and seems to enjoy an un-natural affection for the semi-colon, which he uses to great excess; but, realistically, that is the way they wrote back then. For some reason, in his hand-written text he used a series of six Xs instead of the usual ellipses (…), but not for an omission in the narrative.

Finally, each chapter is preceded by some observations and comments that hopefully put some substance behind the articles or thoughts expressed by the Colonel. It is also set in a context that I trust enhances the enjoyment of the piece. At the end of each article are bullet point biographies of some of the major dramatis personae involved.

I hope you find some historical pleasure in this little book. It gives some insight into the character of a soldier of the British

Empire. With some research, I managed to create a short bullet point biography of his life that now follows.

H.B.

Bullet point biography of James William Caldwell Hutchinson:

- **BORN:** 20th of January 1860 at Saharanpur, Calcutta. His father is a civil surgeon, who later became a Surgeon-General in the Indian army.

- **1871 CENSUS:** Aged 11 and at boarding school in Bristol with his siblings, Emily (15), Constance (12), and Mary (4).

- **ARMY LIST 1879:** Is stationed at York, aged 19, and is a 2nd Lieutenant. In January, he is with the 15th Foot (The Duke of York's Own), and by March is with the 25th Foot, known as the King's Own Borderers, a Scottish regiment.

- **ARMY LIST 1880:** In the month of May he is still at York, but now a Lieutenant in the King's Own Borderers.

- **1881 CENSUS:** Now aged 21 and still a Lieutenant stationed at the New Infantry Barracks, York.

- **ARMY LIST 1882:** In March, he is still a Lieutenant, but is now in the Borders Staff Corps.

- **ARMY LIST 1890:** In January, he was promoted to Captain in the Indian Staff Corps and attached to the 6th Punjab Infantry.

- **1896:** Married Lilian Byrde on December 17th at Keynsham, Bristol. He was 36, she was 21.

- **ARMY LIST 1899:** In January, he is promoted to Major in the Indian Staff Corps.

- **ARMY LIST 1905:** In April, he is promoted to the substantive rank of Lieutenant Colonel.

- **ARMY LIST 1907:** Retired as an invalid on a pension, aged 47. Also, known as a Non-Effective Officer.

- **1911 CENSUS:** Aged 51, along with his wife Lilian aged 35; his son Alexander aged 6; his daughter Sheila aged 4; Mary Start, a house parlour maid aged 16; and Florence Parkhead, domestic nurse, aged 18. At the time of the census, they were all living at Southcott Cottage, Weare Gifford, a village just outside Bideford. There is an inventory extant for Southcott Cottage dated 1907, so they must have moved straight into this house on their return to England. Interestingly, records indicate that they had another son named James Frederick who was born on the 23rd of September 1897 in Bengal. There is no trace of him being in school at that time, so it must be assumed that he died in infancy.

- **AT SOME POINT, AFTER 1911, THEY MOVED TO TOWER HOUSE, ORCHARD HILL, BIDEFORD.**

- **1928:** On the 30th of December, Colonel Hutchinson died of Myocardial degeneration (heart failure) and Arterial Sclerosis (hardening of the arteries.) He was only 67 years of age. It seems that his heart condition could have been the result of the infection picked up in Afghanistan between 1905 and 1907.

- **1929:** His obituary was published in The Western Morning News & Mercury on the 3rd of January, and on the 4th of January in The Western Times. They were virtually identical.

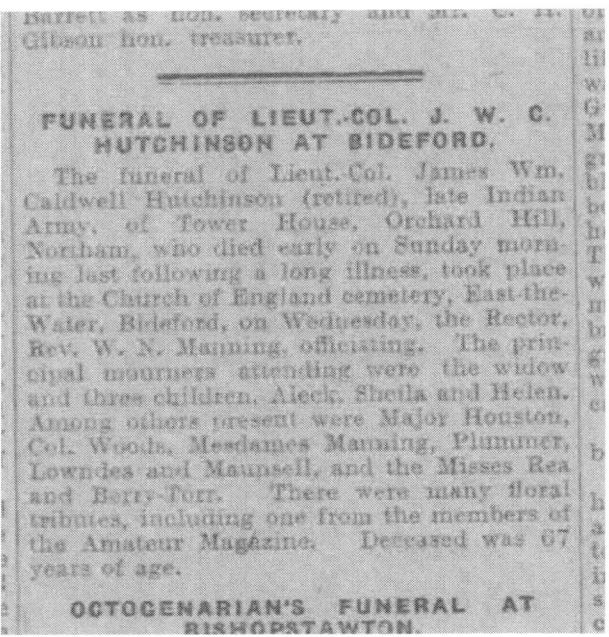

The Western Morning News & Mercury

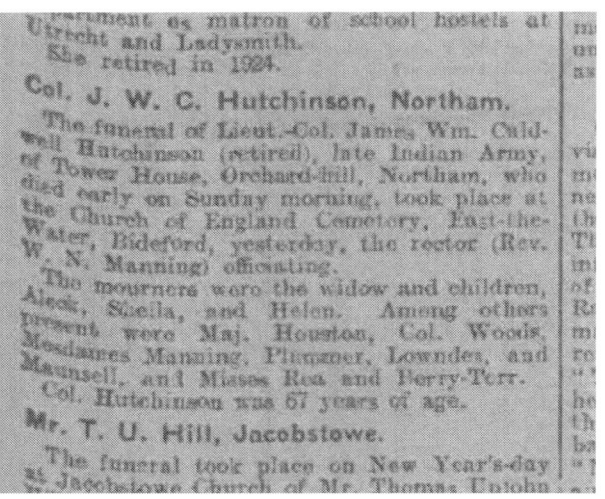

The Western Times

The Colonel's grave at East The Water cemetery, Bideford.

1929: On the 2nd of March, Emily Gertrude Hutchinson and Arthur Thomas Marshall probated his will at Gloucester. His estate came to the value of £951, three shillings, and fourpence. In 2017 that amount would be the equivalent of £54,777 and 60p.

1929 – The Colonel's probated will.

PART 1 – ARTICLES AND OBSERVATIONS MADE ON ACTIVE SERVICE.

1885-1886

"CAMP OF EXERCISE – DELHI 1885-86"

The 25-year-old Lieutenant Hutchinson was stationed on the North-Western Frontier during the "Camp of Exercise" and was witness to an event that could have triggered a major international incident. It centred on Afghanistan, the country that has been a thorn in the flesh of Britain and Russia for many, many, years; much of it self-inflicted by greed.

Billeted in Kohat when news of the incident reached him, Lieutenant Hutchinson reveals himself as a great patriot and empiricist. His proud streak cannot be restrained, as he demonstrates when the British military fails to respond physically to the Russian attack on Afghanistan.

He opens an interesting line of thought regarding the off-hand treatment of Turkey. If they had been invited to the event, it could have had a positive effect and influenced them to side with the Allies instead of the Axis powers during the Great War. If a little more tact and diplomacy was used at this time then Churchill's embarrassment, and the ensuing carnage at the Dardanelle's, could have been avoided.

There is a temptation to think of the British Empire's Army as a well-oiled, smooth running machine, but nothing could be further from the truth. As the incident of the flooded camp illustrates, even back then, people tried to get away with doing as little as possible and then paying the price for it. Or rather, the ordinary man pays the price for it; in this case, it being the unfortunate squaddie and Sepoy.

Lieutenant Hutchinson makes numerous tongue-in-cheek comments about the exercise. He refers to the Northern Army's "victory" over the Southern Army (it was a fix). Then, after showing off Britain's great military strength and skill, came the showing off of its organisation and discipline during ceremonial parades. This collapses into farce during the Great Shoe Incident, which, as is usual in official reports, was greatly glossed over. Only a thunderstorm is mentioned. Such is the power of spin. It's worth noting here that he calls the Viceroy, Paul Dufferin. This is an error. The Viceroy's name was rather more than this. Besides not actually being called Paul, his real full name was, Frederick Temple – Hamilton – Temple – Blackwood, 1st Marquis of Dufferin and Ava.

✒✒✒

I do not suppose many people recollect or are even aware that we almost went to war with Russia in 1885, so I will briefly recapitulate the causes of the quarrel. My account may not be quite accurate as I only kept a meagre diary at the time, but I think that on the whole it is substantially correct.

In 1884 the Russians occupied Merv, and then advanced towards the frontier of Afghanistan; it seemed as if they intended to seize Herat, which had for many years been considered the Gateway to India.

This Russian advance greatly perturbed the Indian Government which came to the conclusion that the best way of arresting it, would be to have the Afghan Frontier clearly delineated. They therefore proposed to the Russian Government, that India and Russia should each despatch a Boundary Commission, who would meet and mutually define the Afghan Frontier. Russia agreed to this proposal.

Late in 1884 our Boundary Commission left India, and making their way through Quetta, Kandahar, and Herat reached the Afghan Frontier not far from the N.E. corner of Persia. The Russian Boundary Commission did not put in an appearance, so our officers found themselves in an awkward position.

The following telegram was published in India on the 23rd February 1885 – 'Russians advancing, Boundary Commission retiring on Herat.' This telegram created a profound sensation in India, and rumours of war filled the air. Later on, two Army Corps with a third in reserve was mobilized on paper, so that if the necessity arose, a strong force could advance without any due delay on Herat. My Regiment was detailed for service with the 1st Army Corps.

Things calmed down on the Afghan Frontier, and our Boundary Commission returned thereto, and encamped in the neighbourhood of a place called Panjdeli. This was a town situated in a fertile strip of territory on the riverbank of the Khushk river. The Russians claimed this piece of ground, and crossing the river on the 30th March, attacked the Afghan Forces garrisoning Panjdeli; these made a brave defence, but were outnumbered and eventually defeated with the loss of their commander and 500 men.

This one-sided fight occurred within sound, if not within sight of the Camp of our Boundary Commission; to add a further point to this insult, a Colonel Alikhanov (a mussulman [*Muslim*] with a Russianised name) rode through our Camp on the evening of the same day with the boots of the Afghan Commissioner slung across his saddlebow. Our Boundary Commission again retired.

The news of this outrage reached Paul Dufferin, the Viceroy of India, on the 8th April at Rawal Pindi, where curiously enough he was entertaining Abdurrahman, the Amir of Afghanistan. This ruler had come at the invitation of the Viceroy to consult with him on affairs of state, and especially with reference to the Russian advance, and the delineation of the Afghan Frontier.

The news was not communicated to the general public in India till the 10th April. On the evening of that day a number of officers of which I was one, were playing cricket at Kohat. The Station Staff Officer came hurrying up; on arrival, he produced a telegram and read it aloud. This was the message – 'Russians attacked Afghans, and killed 500. War with Russia inevitable.' There was a cheer, and then we departed for our several bungalows, to get our service kits ready, as we expected to receive instant orders to march. Those marching orders to our astonishment never came, for Great Britain swallowed the affront! The British and Russian Boundary Commissioners met in July and the Afghan Frontier was finally delineated, but not until our Chief Commissioner had had to travel to St Petersburg to settle some knotty points. Panjdeli was given to the Russians.

English residents in India are apt to forget that there is a huge tribunal of many hundred million people inhabiting the country between the Himalayas and Cape Camorin, who sit in silent judgement on the deeds of their foreign rulers. There is very little doubt that this mighty tribunal came to the conclusion on this occasion that the Sarhar (Indian Government) was afraid to fight the Russlog [*Russians*] and our prestige was considerably lowered in consequence.

The British Lion himself felt that he had cut but a sorry figure in the eyes of the world in allowing his tail to be so badly tweaked without making any attempt at retaliation. He bethought himself that the best way of restoring his damaged reputation would be to make a display of the claws and muscles of his near relative – the Bengal Tiger.

In other words, the British Government decided to show the Great Powers what a powerful weapon they possessed in the Indian Army. A force of 40,000 troops would be assembled during the ensuing cold weather; these would join in mimic warfare, and their manoeuvres would be concluded by the holding of a Grand Review. The Great Powers, Germany, France, Russia, Austria, Italy, and the

United States were each invited to send two officers to witness the manoeuvres. It would have been an act of courtesy to have asked the Lesser European Powers, especially our old ally Turkey to do the same, but it was doubtless deemed that their feelings were not worth considering. Turkey perhaps may have felt the slight, and it might possibly have had some influence on her decision to take up arms against us in 1914.

The Indian Military Authorities took the necessary steps to assemble the Troops. In November 20,000 men were ordered to assemble at Umballa, and were termed the Northern Army, and another force of 20,000 men were ordered to concentrate at Gurgron 25 miles South West of Delhi, and 150 miles from Umballa, and was termed the Southern Army. On a certain date both these armies would advance, and would meet on the historic Battlefield of Panipat, where the fate of India, had previous to our rule been decided on three separate occasions.

The Colonel of my Regiment was ordered to detail an officer to perform the duties of Transport Officer to one of the Brigades of the Northern Army, and as I was the youngest and least useful officer in the Regiment, he selected me for this duty.

Towards the end of November I left for Umballa which I reached in a couple of days. I reported myself to the Chief Transport Officer of the Northern Army, and made the acquaintance of the other Brigade Transport Officers. I struck up a friendship with one of these; he belonged to a Baluchi Regiment and had been with our Boundary Commission, as a special correspondent to 'The Pioneer,' and so was well acquainted with all the exciting episodes that had taken place on the Afghan Frontier during the spring.

We stayed some days in Umballa engaging native writers for our temporary offices, and receiving instruction in the methods of filling up the numerous transport returns that were required. We then proceeded to join the Northern Army which was encamped two marches off.

The camps of the two Divisions comprising the Northern Army were separated by an interval of three or four miles. We remained in these camps for three weeks, whilst the troops were perfecting themselves in fighting tactics. There were many Field days, necessitating the expenditure of much blank ammunition; the results of these Field days were decided by umpires, whose badge of office was a white armlet. These were not selected for their proficiency in military science, but were probably selected for the same reason that I was, viz that they could most easily be spared by their respective Regiments. They were quite a nice lot of fellows, but speedily got themselves disliked for their decisions on the Field of Battle.

It is possible to imagine the feelings of a Colonel, commanding a fire, well-disciplined battalions advancing to the attack in perfect order, when a white arm banded officer galloped up, and greeted him as follows – 'My dear Sir! What *are* you doing? Can't you see those three batteries over there (waving his arm towards the distant horizon) are simply overwhelming you with shrapnel? Please close your battalion, retire 300 paces and lie down;

you must take no further part in the action; your battalion is completely and totally annihilated.'

Some officer propounded the following conundrum, which speedily went the round of the camp, —Why is an umpire like Samson? The answer is so obvious, that the members of the A.M. [*Amateur Magazine*] will probably guess it off hand, but in case some do not care to give themselves the trouble of guessing, here is the answer – 'because he smites thousands with the jawbone of an ass.'

The cold weather in the Punjab is generally a continual succession of fine days; a few gentle showers may be expected about Xmas time. One morning to our surprise a tremendous thunderstorm accompanied by perfect torrents of rain, burst over the camp. The site for this had been selected by intelligent Staff Officers, who did not go to the trouble of taking levels, as the whole country seemed perfectly flat. Water, however informed us that we were pitched on the lowest part of the plain. By the time the rain ceased towards evening, the entire camping ground was covered with about a foot of water. It was rather an unusual experience to have to wade to the Mess Tent for dinner; the reflections of the lights from the hundreds of tents were very picturesque and striking. Dining with water reaching up to our calves was another novel experience. There was no whist after and we all speedily retired to our tents. Officers had camp beds, which just cleared the water, so we were able to sleep in comfort. I don't remember how poor Thomas and the sepoy passed the night; they probably piled up their straw bedding and sat on it.

When I awoke in the morning I was glad to find that the waters had entirely subsided; our tents were just opposite the camp of the 5th Fusiliers, and it struck me that T.A. [*Tommy Atkins*] was unusually lively; there was much shouting and what sounded like the thwacks of sticks. I got up, put some clothes on, and looked out of my tent. I saw the men, here and there, striking at some objects on the ground; these I soon saw were snakes; one biggish chap passed not far from my tent, slithering through the mud, and all covered in slime; he was speedily spotted and despatched. The snakes did not expect the deluge any more than we did and were comfortably hibernating down below, where the water forced them out of their holes.

Nobody seemed to be any the worse for the flood, but a man of the Commissariat Department was actually drowned. He had absorbed more alcohol than was good for him, and falling down was unable to rise.

On the last day of 1885 we commenced our march towards Panipat. The baggage moved along the Grand Trunk Road, which extends from Peshawar to Calcutta; this is probably one of the finest roads in the world. It was very broad, so the transport animals were able to proceed in two or three lines abreast instead of being strung out into one long line. The road was flanked on either hand by broad grass rides, which we transport officers found convenient as they enabled us to avoid riding amidst all the dust kicked up by the baggage animals.

In these days of huge armies, a force of 20,000 men would be looked upon as a mere nothing, but it required an astonishing amount of transport; it was really an impressive sight to see, day after day, what seemed one interminable procession of camels, mules, ponies and carts proceeding along the road.

On the 8th January, the Northern and Southern Armies encountered one another as per programme at Panipat and a furious conflict ensued. These sham fights always degenerate into farce; opposing troops are not allowed to approach within 100 yards of each other, and when that interval is reached, neither side will give way – it is very easy to be brave when there are no bullets flying through the air. Umpires had to gallop about putting troops out of action here, there and everywhere. At last the bugles all down the long line sounded the 'Cease Fire', and the battle of Panipat was over. All the umpires gathered together, and after a lengthy pow-wow, proclaimed that the palm of victory was awarded to the Northern Force.

I have often wondered what would have happened if the umpires had awarded the Southern Army the victory. They would then in that case have completely upset all the arrangements made by the Supreme Authorities. Was there not at Delhi all ready for the Viceroy's accommodation an encampment of huge tents, within a temporary enclosure, laid out tastefully with paths bordered by shrubs and plants innumerable in pots? Had not the commander-in-Chief another magnificent encampment though on a slightly smaller scale? And what of the camps of Lieutenant-Governors and other lesser luminaries? Were not all the arrangements made for the Grand Review to take place at Delhi, the historic capital of India? And last but not least had not woman, lovely woman, who is ever ready to grace any pageant with her beautiful presence, flocked in large numbers to Delhi from every quarter of India? Were all these ladies and notabilities to be inconvenienced and arrangements upset, simply because a number of umpires had chosen to award victory to the Southern Army. The umpires though as I have already written, had sufficient intelligence to understand that the Northern Army should gain the day.

We halted three days after the battle of Panipat to allow the shattered forces of the Southern Army to reform and retreat in comfort. This respite, of course, would never have been given them in real war. The enemy took advantage of the respite to construct a formidable entrenched position outside Delhi, in the neighbourhood of a place named Badli-Ki-Sarai, the scene of a mutiny battle; we reached this position after five days march.
It was a military axiom in those days that an attacking force, in order to take an entrenched position, should be at least three times the strength of the defending force. At the battle of Badli-Ki-Sarai, the attacking and defending forces were of similar strength, so the Northern Army was faced with a hopeless task.

The opening stages of the engagement were spectacular, and I witnessed an imposing charge of North against South Cavalry, but when the infantry attack was held up, the battle degenerated into a farce as usual. I saw attacking infantry trying to dig themselves in, on the open plain while the defending infantry were blazing away at them from behind their entrenchments about 300 yards away.

When the 'Cease Fire' sounded, the umpires had an easy task, and victory was awarded to the Southern Army.

The Great Review was fixed for the 18th January. We had all come to the Camp of Exercise with service kits only, but somewhere on the march from Umballa we had been told that full dress uniform would have to be worn on this grand occasion, so these uniforms had to be sent for.

There was a huge canvas city all about the Northern outskirts of the city of Delhi; and the war being now at an end, the troops of the Northern and Southern Armies fraternized, and we heard something of the foreign officers; they and all the notabilities had accompanied the Southern Army. We were most interested in the two Russian representatives; there were Colonel Prince Odoiovsky of the Cuirassier Guards, and Colonel Timler of the infantry. Odoiovsky (who was christened at once by T.A. [*Tommy Atkins*] as Odour O'whisky) was a fine handsome man with hearty genial manners, and was evidently selected for his social qualities. Timler on the other hand was a sour-faced intelligent looking person, and was clearly the one who had the brains, and who took notes of all he thought worth recording.

One of the U.S. officers was a very indifferent rider, and on one occasion was given a rather restive mount. His fellow representative remarked to the British Officer who had been detailed to look after the welfare of the Foreign Officers – 'That horse is playing cup and ball with my partner, and I guess the cup is going to miss the ball in a minute or two.' His prediction proved correct, for his partner suddenly found himself seated with violence on the ground.

In the days of which I am writing, great attention was paid to what were known as 'Ceremonial Parades' and an Infantry Battalion which could march past like a wall was looked upon with much favour. All the troops comprising the North and South Armies were especially picked for their efficiency and smartness, and the Military Authorities felt confident that they would make a splendid show before the Foreign Officers, who would of course report to their respective Governments what a magnificent Army we had in India. But 'man proposes and God disposes.'

The morning of the 18th broke dark and lowering, and by the time the troops had formed on the Parade Ground the weather looked very threatening indeed. The Viceroy accompanied by a magnificent staff, and the Foreign Officers rode onto the ground. As he reached the Saluting Flag, the first gun of a Regal Salute thundered out. This was answered at once by a dazzling flash from the sky, and a report which quite eclipsed man's feeble artillery. Then down came the rain in an absolute deluge, which soon soaked everybody to the skin, damaged, if not ruined light coloured uniforms, and turned the Parade Ground into a morass.

It was thought that the Viceroy should have dismissed the Parade at once, and he probably would have done so, had it not been for the presence of the Foreign Officers, but it was said that he did not wish them to think that our troops were afraid of the rain. He probably, a little later on, regretted that he had not dismissed the Parade; for had he done so, the Great Shoe Incident, which turned the Grand Review into something resembling a fiasco, would not have occurred.

I must make a digression to explain the nature of this incident.

The Sepoy was not in my time, supplied like Thomas Atkins, with an absolutely full kit, but he received instead on enlisting a sum of 30 Rupees, and a yearly allowance of five Rupees, which sums were supposed to cover the cost and maintenance of all his uniform with the exception of a cloth tunic and breeches, which were renewed periodically. These pecuniary allowances were called 'Half Mounting.' The origins of this strange word I have never been able to discover; it is probably the corruption of some word used in the early days of the rule of the East India Company. The Half Mounting allowance was not sufficient to pay for all the articles of a Sepoy's kit, consequently some of them had to be paid for by the Sepoy himself. The Punjabi Sepoy is a thrifty soul and used to take great interest in his Half Mounting account, which was read out and explained to him monthly. If his account was on the Debit side, he was unhappy because he realised that if he lost or damaged any article of his kit, he would have to replace it at his own cost.

Sepoys in Punjab Regiments love the native shoe, in which they simply slipped their feet, as the shoe was not laced. These shoes were an excellent foot-gear for the dry climate of the Punjab and answered capitally on the rocky hills of the Frontier, as they were much lighter than boots.

When the March Past commenced the whole Parade Ground was a sea of mud, and this mud sucked any number of shoes from off their owner's feet. The cost of these shoes was 1.4 Rupees per pair, rather less than $1/5^{th}$ of the Sepoy's pay of 7 Rupees per month. A number of men, probably those whose Half Mounting accounts were on the debit side, as soon as they lost a shoe or shoes in the mud, broke the ranks and went back to recover their missing property, and there was much confusion. One Regiment in particular must have had particularly loose fitting shoes, for the men ran back in scores. The Colonel of the regiment, as well as the Regiment itself incurred the severe displeasure of the Commander-in Chief.

I believe the pay of the Commander-in-Chief used to be 10,000 Rupees per month; if he had lost an article to the value of 1,850 Rupees on that Parade Ground, he might possibly have made an attempt to recover it. 1.4 Rupees sounds a mere bagatelle, but the loss of this small sum meant as much to the Sepoy as the loss of 1,850 Rupees would have meant to the Commander-in-Chief.

I cannot speak as an eyewitness of the truth of the shoe incident, as I was not present at the Parade; my full-dress uniform did not reach me in time; but there is no doubt that the scramble for the missing shoes did actually occur, and that all the Great Powers must have been duly informed of it by their representatives.

There is however no mention of the shoe incident, either in the "Life of Lord Dufferin" written by Sir A. Lyall, nor in "Forty-One Years in India" written by Lord Roberts.

Lord Dufferin wrote to the Secretary of State for India as follows –
'Though the glitter of the spectacle was dimmed, the sight was splendid. One forgot the storm and everything else in one's interest in looking at the men. Indeed, from a business point of view I am not sure but what it was better as it was, as it enabled our soldiers to show what pluck and discipline could effect in adverse circumstances. Though they were almost up to their knees in mud, each battalion marched past like a straight solid wall. The ground was especially trying to our poor little, short-legged Ghurkhas; but they ground their teeth and set their faces, and passed the Saluting Flag in as level a line as any other Regiment.'

Ghurkhas wore boots which of course did not come off in the mud.

Lord Roberts wrote –
'It was a fine sight, though marred by a heavy thunderstorm, and a perfect deluge of rain, and was really a greater test of what the troops could do, than if we had the perfect weather we had hoped for.'

After having ruined the Grand Review, the weather again became beautifully fine, and a great assault at arms and various festivities took place, after which the troops dispersed.

1886

"DELHI"

After the Camp of Exercise, the young officer Hutchinson stayed on and took in the sights of Delhi. From these he produces a form of travelogue and writes at some length of the famous 1857 Indian Mutiny, and even evinces his own kind of spin on some of the events. He is very disparaging of the mutineers.

During this travelogue, the Colonel gives a rather different version of events surrounding his uncle John Hutchinson and the beginning of the mutiny. The official history indicates that when the British heard that the mutineers were coming Captain Douglas, Commandant of the Palace Guard, Simon Frazer, the Commissioner, Mr Nixon, Frazer's Head Clerk, and John Ross Hutchinson who held the position of Magistrate, went out to meet them at the Bridge of Boats that is adjacent to the Calcutta Gate. I am not sure which of Douglas, as Commandant, Frazer, as Commissioner, or Hutchinson, as Magistrate, would have been the lead negotiator at this point. Before things could progress though, the party was attacked by a band of five Sewers (cavalry troopers) who fired into them. Hutchinson was hit in the arm and the group broke up.

Douglas and Hutchinson escaped by hiding for a while in the ditch that surrounded the Red Fort. During the evasive action, Douglas badly hurt his back and feet. Finally, with the aid of Douglas' servants the two of them managed to return to the rooms at the Lahore Gate where Douglas had his quarters. But this was no safety. Shortly thereafter, the mutineers overrun the apartments and the officials were massacred, including Colonel Hutchinson's uncle. Which is the most accurate version of events, we shall probably never know.

Regarding the rest of the narrative, there are a couple of observations. Firstly, during the colonel's visit to the Peacock Throne he does miss-quote the actual Persian inscription which properly reads – "If there be a paradise on earth, it is this! It is this! It is this! – Three times for emphasis. Secondly, the incident of the pictures for the Regimental Sports Day programme, and the reactions to them, clearly demonstrate in a most unambiguous way the moral hypocrisy of the Victorian and Edwardian age.

🖋 🖋 🖋

After the troops had dispersed on the conclusion of the manoeuvres described in my last article, the Transport Officers stayed on for some time to complete returns, and settle up accounts. The office work did not take up much of each day and I devoted its remainder to sight-seeing, generally in the company of the Baluchi officer.

Our tents were pitched quite near the famous ridge, some 60 feet in height to which our little Army had clung with such heroic tenacity all through those terrible three months in 1857, at the very worst season of the year.

I always think that the Siege and Capture of Delhi, is the most desperate feat of arms, ever carried to a successful issue in the annals of war. It was not really a siege for the city measured seven miles in circumference, and the strength of our small force only enabled it to attack the Northern Force, which was about a mile in length. When this small force first reached Delhi, it numbered 3000 men, while the mutineers within the fortified city numbered 8000 and had the assistance of all the lawless inhabitants which are to be found in every large town.

The numbers of the enemy were being continually swelled by other mutinous Regiments, which were able to make their way into the city without let or hindrance from our troops, who were more besieged than besieging. The rebels had also the advantage of having at their disposal a practically unlimited supply of guns and ammunition contained in the vast magazine, which we had so foolishly entrusted to the native garrison of Delhi long before the outbreak of the mutiny.

Hardly a day passed without our soldiers having to repel fierce attacks by overwhelming numbers of the enemy on their Front, Right Flank, and sometimes even their Rear. Only the Left Flank of our position was fairly secure from attack as it was protected by the River Jumna.

All this fierce fighting took place under the fiery rays of the Indian midsummer sun, and the only head protection our men had, were white cotton covers to their forage caps, with perhaps a small curtain of similar material descending therefrom to protect the nape of the neck. Many men were of course struck down by the sun, but it is marvellous that there was not a much greater mortality on this account.

The sufferings of the sick and wounded were terrible; they had to be accommodated in the ordinary soldiers tents, and as there were no beds, they had to lie on the ground; the worst cases alone were placed in dhulis. They were not only tortured by the heat, but by a dreadful plague of flies, and their nerves were jarred by the almost incessant cannonade and rattle of musketry near at hand. There were no gentle nurses to minister to their every want; recovery from amputation was rare and all wounds healed with difficulty so polluted was the atmosphere of the camp, by the numerous bodies of the mutineers who had been killed close to our defences; our men were so overworked that they were unable to bury these, nor were they able to bury or burn all the carcasses of animals that were killed or died in camp. Cholera and dysentery were rife, but providentially the former terrible disease never assumed the proportions of an epidemic.

Our small army though it suffered heavy casualties both in battle and from disease was gradually reinforced from the Punjab till its numbers rose about the beginning of September to about 8000 men, but the city was then garrisoned by about 35,000 mutineers. With the aid of a siege train two practicable breaches were made in the walls. In spite of the enormous disparity in numbers Delhi was assaulted on the 14th September by four tiny columns and totalling about 4000 men in all. Three of the columns won their way into the city, but the fourth was beaten back.

At the end of the day we had only managed to capture the northern face of the city, with the loss of 1170 men killed and wounded. We persevered in the task, and the whole of Delhi finally fell into our hands on the 20th September.

The services of those magnificent veterans who captured Delhi, and thereby saved India were not sufficiently recognised, and I believe that there is not in this country a single memorial to the gallant British soldiers who laid down their lives so freely at Delhi, Lucknow, Cawnpore and elsewhere.

A walk of a few minutes from our tents took us to the Flag Staff Tower on the Ridge. In this tower, the survivors of the massacre on that dreadful 11th May had taken refuge, waiting for succour by the English troops at Meerat, but that succour never came. Towards evening our poor people started some riding, some driving, and some walking for Meerat or Umballa. They did not commence their long and perilous journeys a moment to soon, for very shortly after they had left, a huge mob of all the ruffianly scum of Delhi surged over the Ridge and burnt every bungalow in the Station.

It was possible to see, from the top of the Flag Staff Tower, practically all the positions held by our troops during the siege, and the Northern face of the City as well. About a mile to the south of the town, and almost at the extremity of the Ridge, stood Hindu Rao's house; this had been the key to our position, and had been held throughout the Siege by the Sirmur battalion of Ghurkhas, aided by two Companies of the 60th Rifles, and later by the Ghurkha Infantry. The house was within easy gun range of the City Wall, and was riddled through and through with shot and shell. Between Hindu Rao's house and the Flag Staff Tower stands the memorial to the officers and men who lost their lives during the siege.

A road passes through the ridge close to the Flag Staff Tower, and a walk of about 1 ½ miles brings one to the Kashmir Gate. This Gate was blown in on the 14th September by our gallant explosion party. The members of the Amateur Magazine are probably well acquainted with the deeds of this heroic little band, so I will merely state that the mutineers had removed the bridge across the 30 feet wide ditch all except the two side beams, and over these beams, our men laden with powder bags had to cross in broad daylight. They succeeded in blowing in the Gate, but nearly all the party were either killed or wounded.

In 1886 the walls through which the Kashmir gate passed were in the identical shot-battered condition they were in on the actual day of the assault: perhaps they may be so still. The Gate has a double entrance, and between the two entrances, there was a large marble slab, on which were recorded the names and deeds of the explosion party.

Within the City, and quite close to the Kashmir Gate stood the Delhi Church; this was an imitation of St Paul's Cathedral on a small scale. The cross and ball which surmounted the dome at the time of the siege were kept as relics in the Church garden; the ball was riddled by bullets, which the mutineers had fired at it for [a] pastime, and for the sake of destroying the emblems of our religion, but strange to say, the cross was almost, if not completely undamaged by the mutineer's bullets. Inside the Church, there is a tablet to the memory of an uncle of mine, who at the time of the mutiny was Collector and Magistrate of Delhi. Hearing on the morning of the 11th May the approach of the rebel cavalry from Meerat, he rode across the bridge of boats over the Jumna to try and dissuade them from entering the City; needless to say he was cut down almost at once. His wife with two tiny children escaped from the city in a dhubi, to the Flag Staff Tower, after having been fired at on the way. She with her children eventually succeeded in reaching Meerat, and later a safer refuge in the Himalayas. She remained long in ignorance of her husband's death, hoping against hope that he had affected his escape to some other asylum.

Close to the Western Wall of the city and about ¾ of a mile from the Kashmir Gate is the spot, where John Nicholson fell mortally wounded, when leading an attack up a narrow lane on the Burn Bastion. He lingered in great agony for nine days, before death relieved him of his sufferings.

Nicholson had arrived at Delhi about a month before the assault, and it is supposed that his influence and determination largely contributed towards the decision of the General to deliver the assault. If Delhi had not fallen when it did, it is very probable that the Sikhs would have risen, and thrown in their lot with the mutineers, and we should have lost India.

Nicholson was of commanding stature and a born ruler of men, but his imperious bearings and reserved manner made him somewhat unpopular with those who did not know him well; he was however adored by those who did know and understand him. His name was a household word amongst the natives of the Northern Punjab, and we read that it was a pathetic sight to witness the grief of the wild Frontier Chieftains and fierce Multani horsemen, when they heard of his death. Even stout-hearted John Lawrence, who had done more than anyone else to help crush the mutiny, and whose orders Nicholson had on occasion disobeyed when marching to Delhi, is said to have shed tears when the sad news reached him. The natives regarded him as a sort of demi-god, and some formed themselves into a sect under the name of 'Nikkul Seynees', and actually worshiped him. Whenever Nicholson caught any of this sect worshipping him he gave the worshipper a good sound flogging, but this did not deter the sect from continuing to look upon him as their patron Saint.

Apart from the interest attached to Delhi, because it was the scene of the greatest struggle during the mutiny, there is much in the way of historical association as well as architecture to attract the visitor.

Neither my friend nor I knew anything of architecture, but we visited the Palace and Jama Majid both built by the Emperor Shah Jahan in the 17th Century.

The palace is enclosed within walls 40 feet in height, and 1 ½ miles in circuit. It contains the Halls of Public and Private Audience; the former is built of red sandstone, and the latter entirely of polished marble. In the centre of the Hall of Private Audience used to stand the famous Peacock Throne, made of solid gold and studded with precious stones; it was carried off by the Persian Conqueror Nadir Shah in 1739. In the same Hall there is an inscription in Persian – "If there is a Paradise on earth, it is this! It is this!"

Within the Palace enclosure there is also the exquisite 'Moti Majid' or 'Pearl Mosque' built of polished marble.

Some distance to the South of the Palace, stands the great Jama Majid, which is the largest mosque in India. The materials used in its construction are red sandstone and white marble. The mosque is flanked by two minarets each about 140 feet high.

When the Baluchi officer and I visited the Jama Majid, there was a large crowd of worshippers, as it happened to be one of the five appointed times of prayer during the day. We climbed the spiral staircase of a minaret, and watched the scene from the top. The different motions observed during prayer time were all done in unison, and rather reminded one of a drill, but the greatest solemnity and reverence were observed by each worshipper. The congregation from a standing position sank to their knees, and after two or three minutes spent in kneeling they bent forwards till their foreheads touched the ground; this was done several times, when the kneeling posture was resumed, and then the standing. After an interval the whole procedure was gone through again and again, for I do not know how many times.

The day before we left Delhi we visited the Kutab Minar, which stands about nine miles to the South of Delhi. There are ruins on every hand; the ruins of old Delhi are said to cover 20 square miles of surface; amongst them are various tombs of the Mogul Emperors; the best known one being that of Humayun, which is 400 yards square.

The Kutab is 240 feet high, and is I believe, the tallest masonry pillar in the world. The base is 100 feet and the top 30 feet in circumference. We ascended to the top to admire the view.

It is not known why the Kutab was built, but there is a tradition that it was erected by an ancient King of Delhi, who desired to give a favourite wife a glimpse of her beloved Ganges from the summit.

About 40 feet below the top a little balcony about two feet wide encircles the tower; the balcony has a knee-high balustrade. On our descent, the Baluchi officer passed through a little door onto the balcony, and then started walking round it; I followed suit, fortunately we both had good heads, and got around quite quickly; there are altogether four balconies encircling the tower at irregular intervals.

Not far from the base of the Kutab, there stands a solid iron pillar 60 feet high; the origin of this is also lost in mystery, but a

Hindu legend states that the base of the pillar rests on the dragon which supports the Earth.

While inspecting the ruins, we were pestered by a number of boys who wanted us to see them dive; we rather jeered at them as there did not seem to be any water for them to dive into. They, however, conducted us to a well, not the ordinary type of narrow circular well, but one of hexagonal form, the breadth between opposite sides being about 30 feet. There were some half-a-dozen stone galleries all-round the interior of the well. We descended by steps to the lowest gallery, which was almost on a level with the water, this was green in colour, and did not look attractive. The boys however had no objections to the stagnant water, and jumped into it, feet foremost one after the other from the top of the well, a height of about 60 feet. They were quite content with a few small coins, with which we rewarded them. This well was probably used in far distant days, as a refuge from the heat of the upper air.

The next day the Baluchi officer and I left Delhi, travelling together as far as Lahore, where we separated; he had to go South and I North.

When I reached Kohat, I learnt that our Regimental Sports were due to take place in two or three weeks. It was known that I possessed the knack of drawing figures of sorts, though I had no knowledge of either art or anatomy, and the Colonel asked me to prepare an illustrated programme, which would be circulated amongst the all the Residents of the Station and so acquaint them with the nature of the various events etc.

I had no drawing paper, and as there did not happen to be a shop for the sale of artists materials in Kohat, I had to content myself with a sheet of plain foolscap. I drew on the front page a couple of Sikhs racing towards the spectator. I depicted them running in the exact attire that Sikh runners would use on the day of the sports. This attire was of a rather light description and consisted of nothing but a loin cloth and comb.

I will make a slight digression here to explain that a boy born of Sikh parents is not a Sikh till he takes the Sikh oath about the age of 15. He swears to live by the sword, and never to allow any of his hair to be cut. The hair of his head is twisted in coils, and kept in place by a comb, while the ends of the beard are twisted around the ears.

On the back of the programme I drew three or four small sketches depicting various events, and in the centre I wrote out the programme itself as neatly as I could. The Colonel and Officers were good enough to be pleased with the result, and the Adjutant was directed to have the programme circulated amongst the residents. The next morning a sepoy started taking them round. The same morning, after having finished what Regimental work I had to do, I returned to my bungalow, changed into plain clothes, and sat down in my easy chair to enjoy a book. I heard someone ride up to the front of the bungalow, and a minute or two later the Adjutant with some papers in his hands walked into the room; he came up to my chair, and with his arms akimbo, surveyed me in silence for a few seconds.

"Well young fellow!" he said to me at length, "You have been and gone and done it! I think I ought to put you under arrest!"

"What have I been doing?" I asked not at all perturbed by his threat, as I had quite an easy conscience, and had besides noticed a distinct twinkle in his eye.

"You have been trying to corrupt the morals of the good people of Kohat by circulating indecent pictures."

"What do you mean?" I again asked.

"I'll shew you the filthy pictures you have been sending round to everyone in the Station," and the Adjutant produced my unhappy programme, and held it before my face. "The men you have drawn are almost as good as naked."

"I have shewn them just as they will run at the sports" I replied "and the Colonel saw and approved of the pictures before they were sent round."

"Yes, but he had no idea, what delicate feelings some of the ladies of the Station possess. Just read this letter which he received a few minutes ago."

The Adjutant handed the letter over to me. It was written by X – an officer of the garrison. As far as I can recollect he wrote that my pictures had deeply shocked his wife's sense of propriety, and they were not fit to be sent round for ladies to see.

"Why" I said, "Mrs X came to the 3rd Sikh's sports only last week, and did not appear to be at all shocked at the very slight costume worn by the runners."

"Yes, I know she did, but these things look different on paper. Besides, when you have lived as long as I have (he was only three or four years my senior) you will understand that the members of the fair sex are creatures of moods. If Mrs X had seen that programme of yours yesterday, she would probably have gone into raptures over it, but today she finds it shocking. The colonel though does not wish to receive any more letters of this type, so would you just make out an ordinary programme undecorated with improper pictures!"

I consented, and he took his departure. I commenced writing out a new programme wondering all the while over the ways of Mrs X, and whether the generality of her sex were creatures of moods.

The day of the sports arrived, and as it happened, the Russian officers Colonel Prince Odoiovsky and Colonel Timler, who were making a tour under the care of an officer were expected to arrive at Kohat in the afternoon.

The sports were attended by all the English residents, as well as by practically all the native officers and men of the garrison, so there was a great crowd. Mrs X turned up, looking quite happy, and sat with other ladies perhaps a dozen in number, just by the winning post. So she had a close view of the almost naked runners.

Rather late in the afternoon, the Russian officers with their bear leader appeared on the ground. Just then an open event for the

Mountain Battery, and a very popular and spectacular one was commencing.

The conditions of the contest were as follows:- the teams of the six guns of the Battery were drawn up along a certain line (the teams besides the gunners and drivers, consisted for four mules, three of these carried the gun, carriage, and wheels, while the fourth was loaded with a pair of ammunition boxes). At the pistol shot all the six gun teams were to advance to a second line, 50 yards in front, where the guns were to be unlimbered, and then wheeled by hand another 50 yards up to a third line, the first gun which fired a round of blank cartridge after reaching this line would win the contest.

At that time the Punjabi Frontier Force batteries were not armed with the screw gun, which is carried in two parts, but had the old fashioned seven pounders, carried in one piece, and irreverently termed a pop-gun. I have forgotten now the exact time it took a gun detachment to get the gun, carriage, and wheels off their respective mules, and put them together, all ready for action, but it was a matter of seconds, about 48 I believe, so smart were the gunners.

The teams lined up, as I have described, then off went the pistol; the gun teams hurried up to the first line, where the guns were unlimbered, and put together, and then they were trundled by hand up to the third line. Five guns reached this line one after the other, but number one gun was distinctly behind-hand. I was standing a few paces to the right of this gun, and saw at once that the crew were unduly excited. Some hitch had probably occurred in unlimbering and the men were trying to make up for lost time. The gunner, who had brought up the cartridge from the ammunition mule instead of returning to his place in rear, remained in front of the gun, waving his arms in wild excitement, and trying to hasten up his fellows.

All the other five guns had fired, and I was calling out to number one gun not to fire, when bang went the gun; the ammunition carrier appeared to rise in the air, with his arms close to his sides, and his legs held stiff and straight together just like a toy wooden soldier, and then fell heavily flat along the ground. The rammer had caught him on the side of the head, and he was killed on the spot. The gun-crew had gone all to pieces with excitement; as soon as the cartridge was rammed home, the gunner whose duty it was to fire the gun, had placed the friction tube in the vent, and pulled the cord attached to the tube; fortunately for himself, the man who rammed had seen that he was about to fire, so let go of the rammer, otherwise he would have had his arms blown off, but the poor ammunition carrier, who should have been in the rear, was killed.

Our Colonel stopped the sports on the occurrence of this dreadful incident; which was ascribed by all the natives to the malign presence of the Russians. They both however contributed very handsomely to a fund raised for the deceased man's widow and orphans.

The Russian officers dined at our Garrison Mess in the evening; the married officers, and the few civilians in the place, all came to do them honour, so we were a very large party.

When the P.F.F. [Punjab Frontier Force] was first raised in 1849, it was termed the Punjab Irregular Force, and it probably was very irregular indeed, so much so that the officers did not wear uniforms at mess; this ancient custom was still observed at Kohat. Strangely enough we did not wear the regulation evening clothes in place of uniform, but morning coats and dark trousers. The Russian officers, though they must have been accustomed to almost live in uniform, conformed to our custom, and appeared dressed as ourselves. They looked, I am afraid rather like a pair of commercial travellers. Poor Odoiovsky must have felt sad at not being able to wear his magnificent uniform of the Cuirassier Guards.

Kohat was the only place on the Frontier that the Russians were allowed to see, for they left the following day by the way they had come, through Rawl Pindi and Khushalgash.

With this departure, the incident of the Delhi Camp of Exercise was finally closed, as far as I was concerned.

(AFTERTHOUGHT)

With this note, Colonel Hutchinson corrects a miss-conception he had concerning an event in Delhi during the uprising on 1857. It refers to the above chapter about Delhi.

I was under the impression that the telegraph signallers at Delhi were all murdered on the 11th May. But only one, Todd was murdered. Pilkington and Brendish who was the signaller to actually despatch the famous message survived. In 1902, Lord Curzon when Viceroy, gave Brendish the medal of the Victcrian Order, on the occasion of the unveiling of a monument erected to commemorate the services of the Delhi Telegraphic staff

Bullet Point Biography of John Ross Hutchinson

- **1822:** Born September the 12th in Burdwan, Bengal, India.
- **1839:** Baptised in India.
- **1840-1841:** Attended the East India College in Hertfordshire, now known as Haileybury College.
- **Career path:** Became the Magistrate of Delhi.
- **1857:** Killed during the Indian Mutiny. (See memorial below.)

There is a slight conflict of opinion between the colonel and official reports, and this is discussed in the introduction to the article.

Bullet Point Biography of Brigadier General John Nicholson

- **1822:** Born on the 11th of December at Lisburn, Northern Ireland.
- **Education:** To begin with, he was educated privately at Delgany, and then latterly at the "Royal School," or Dunganon College as it was known.
- **1839:** At the age of 17 he was gifted a cadetship in the Bengal Infantry by his uncle, Sir James Hogg.
- **1839-1842:** The young John Nicholson was instantly involved in the First Afghan War and distinguished himself during the defence of Ghazni. During this time, he met Sir Henry Lawrence who commissioned him to be the political officer of Kashmir, and later of the north-west frontier of the Punjab.
- **1847:** Nicholson was also given charge of the Sind Sagar district, which lay to the east of the north-west frontier, and to the south of Kashmir.
- **1848-1849:** The Second Sikh War broke out and he was heavily involved with that. He eventually became the deputy commissioner of Bannu. It was during this time that the natives began to revere him as a god. It appears that this continued to exist in the remotest rural parts of north-west Pakistan until well into the 1980s.
- **1857:** When the mutiny broke out he almost single-handedly kept the Punjab loyal. For this he was promoted to brigadier general. Later Nicholson and 2,500 troops marched through flooded territory to defeat 6000 sepoys in a battle that lasted for about one hour. On his arrival at Delhi, he led an attack on the Kashmir Gate

with 1000 men. His troops took the gate but Nicholson was mortally wounded by being shot in the back. He hung on for nine days before dying of his wounds on the 23rd of September.

Bullet Point Biography of John Laird Mair Lawrence. Baronet

- **1811:** Born 4th of March at Richmond, North Yorkshire.
- **Education:** Childhood spent at Derry, Northern Ireland. Went to Foyle College at Londonderry, and then to the East India Company College (Haileybury College.)
- **1829:** Went to India with his brother Henry Montgomery Lawrence. In Delhi, he became a magistrate and a collector of taxes.
- **1841:** Married Harriette Katherine Hamilton.
- **1845-1846:** During the First Sikh War, his organisational skills made sure that that supplies reached the British forces stationed in the Punjab. He was awarded the commissionership of the Jullundur district. His brother just happened to be the Governor of the province at the time, so there is a strong sniff of nepotism in the air. Still he was good administrator and kept the hill tribes under control. He tried to end the Hindu custom of suttee (or sati,) but was unsuccessful.
- **1849:** After the Second Sikh War, he totally reorganised the internal administration and infrastructure of the Punjab.
- **1857:** Lawrence helped to prevent the rebellion seeping into the Punjab. He later led the army that recaptured Delhi from the insurrectionists. For this action, he was made a baronet, making him 1st Baron Lawrence. He also got paid a handsome pension from his "employer," the East India Company, of £2000 annually,

a tidy sum at that time. (The equivalent of £197,000 in 2017 values.)

- **1859:** Returned to Britain.
- **1863:** Returned to India for a six-year tenure as Viceroy.
- **1869:** Came back to Britain and was given a peerage making him Baron Lawrence of the Punjab and Grately (a small town in Hampshire.)
- **1879:** Died aged 68.

1890

"A PATHAN JOKE"

While Captain Hutchinson was attached to the Bombay Staff Corps in the 6th Punjab Infantry, he was part of the Punjab Frontier Force. Because of this, he would have been well acquainted with the Pathan tribes and their characteristics, including their sense of humour. This seems to indicate that he had a soft spot for them.

If the Colonel was writing this memoir in the late 1920s, and the incident occurred around the 1890 period, it would have been contemporary to his time there. Probably, he would have been one of the officers involved in this amusing escapade.

The larger histories of India bring us the big picture and large sweep of the international canvas, but the personal experiences of the man in the saddle reveal the details that make up the big picture. A Pathan Joke is a magical little happening that brings to life the human side of the Indian army at that time.

In conclusion, whilst Captain Hutchinson demonstrated appreciation for the joke, it seems that the General was of the old school and possessed a challenged sense of humour.

🖋 🖋 🖋

The Pathan is generally a cheery, though treacherous rascal, but when trained and disciplined he proves a very efficient soldier. Even in his wild state he possesses certain qualities which are attractive to the Englishman; one of which is his capacity for appreciating a joke.

Thirty or forty years ago, when comparatively few breech loading rifles had found their way across the border, it was the Pathan's greatest ambition to obtain one by fair means or foul, as the fortunate owner of an accurate rifle had, in the blood feuds so common amongst frontier tribesmen, an enormous advantage over an enemy, only armed with a country made jezail.

The Pathan was therefore an expert rifle thief, and was also addicted to the habit of stealing lead, so much so in fact, that at Frontier Stations a guard had to be mounted on all rifle ranges, to prevent him and his brethren from digging out all the bullets fired into the butts. Having been thus deprived of this easy method of obtaining free lead, Pathan's had to avail themselves of the casual opportunities offered for picking up scraps of metal, when companies, battalions, and sometimes the whole garrison of a station practiced Field Firing. They always managed to ascertain the dates of such events, and used to gather like vultures round a carcass, in the vicinity of the scene of operations. When the "Cease Fire" had been sounded, and the native soldiers had collected as many fragments of bullets, as they could find amongst the stones, the hill men dashed down, and searched frantically for any lead that had been overlooked.

On one occasion, the General commanding the Punjab Frontier Force, on his annual tour of inspection, had the whole garrison of a certain station out to practice Field Firing. The position selected for the attack was on the slopes of the outer fringe of the border hills. The targets (canvas screens) were put up, and the ground cleared of the usual crowd of Pathan lead stealers, who took cover as near as they could to the positions.

The Brigade drawn up some 1½ miles away, advanced to the attack in the stereotyped fashion of those days, every man doing his best under the eyes of the General. Fire was about to be opened, when all the targets suddenly began to retire up the hillside. Field glasses were brought into play, and the nature of this unusual phenomenon was speedily revealed. Pathan's were furnishing the motive power by carrying the targets up the hill; in their dirty grey garments so similar in colour to the stony slopes, they were quite invisible to the naked eye.

These hill savages were aware of the presence of the General, and evidently arranged their little surprise for his especial benefit, thinking he might enjoy it as much as they did themselves.

The General though, was of a somewhat choleric disposition, and thought at first he would avail himself of this splendid opportunity to exercise the troops in moving target practice, but fearing complications, he despatched instead some cavalry to bring back the errant targets. This was soon done; a party was then detailed to prevent a repetition of the joke, and the Field Firing was duly carried out.

1892

"BANNU TO HUNZA"

This is the travelogue of an epic journey. The Captain has a change of posting from the hot plains to the cool mountains. Along the way, he describes the highly contrasting and varied terrain over which he has to traverse. It covers high mountain ridges and passes, through low valley floors and plains. At one point, his progress was rapid thanks to some native animal amphetamines. The ponies travelled 65 miles in 12 ½ hours, an average speed of 5.2 miles per hour. It was also on this journey where he encountered the inspiring edifice of Mount Rakipushi, an experience that seems to have affected him for the rest of his life.

During his travels, he meets some famous people and name-drops shamelessly. He introduces us to Fenton Aylmer, the prolific Royal Engineer bridge builder who won the Victoria Cross during the Hunza-Nagar expedition of December 1891. Although he does get the details wrong – see Aylmer's bullet point biography. We also come across Sir Charles Townshend who was one of the old school with stiff standards of dress. A modern example of this type of character would be the man who wears a jacket and tie even at the height of a heat wave. Townshend was the Commander of the army who surrendered the Iranian city of Kut in 1916. He overstretched himself and his supply lines.

Disease was rife during this period. Cholera was pandemic it seems. It is interesting to note the way the Colonel demonstrates his superior attitude towards the natives by how he refers to them. It is also shown on the occasion where his servant appeared to be suffering from cholera. The sheer relief expressed when it turns out to be 'just' malaria is palpable. Of course, it is not through any sympathy for his poor bearer, but more for himself, cholera is contagious, but malaria is not!

One final comment on this article; the split in the administration is intriguing. It seems that in India, if you worked for the government you were a 'political' and if you were a member of the armed forces you were classified as a 'military.'

🖋 🖋 🖋

In July 1892, when stationed in Bannu, I was asked by the Military Authorities at Simla, whether I would accept an appointment in the Gilgit district to train Kashmir Imperial Service Infantry and local levies. The work sounded attractive, the pay was good, there was splendid Markor and Ibex shooting about Gilgit, but the greatest inducement of all was the prospect of serving in a cool climate instead of the heat of the plains. I had no hesitation therefore in accepting the appointment.

Early in September, I heard privately from a friend at Simla, that I should soon receive my orders to proceed to Gilgit, so despatched my servants, mare, and baggage to Baramida, there to await my arrival. About a fortnight later I received orders to go to

Srinagar, and report myself to the Resident of Kashmir for further orders.

A brother officer, Captain Browning was leaving at the same time to bring his wife down from Murree which was undergoing a terrible visitation from cholera, and we arranged to travel together as far as Rawal Pindi.

Four or five years previously a very good road had been made between Kohat and Bannu, so every Regiment invested in a Tonga. A certain number of the transport mules were broken to harness, and though they had distinctly hard mouths, they were quite as fast as ponies. Officers could in consequence travel in comfort, instead of having to ride along a very indifferent track.

Towards the end of August, a small force had left Bannu to seize a place named Jhandola in Waziristan, and build a fortified post. Owing to the move of this force, there were only a few mules left in Bannu, and of these two pairs alone could go in harness, so Browning and I would be able to do but two stages of our journey in a tonga.

We decided to drive the remaining 65 miles to Kohat in 'ekkas'. An ekka is a light native pony cart; the sitting accommodation is on a level with the shafts, and is only about four feet square. A native does not mind this, as he is accustomed to the squatting position, but for a European the accommodation is decidedly limited. This difficulty though is solved by having a short, broad plank lashed to one of the shafts as a leg rest, and with the aid of pillows and 'razais' (native quilts) to sit on, it is possible to travel quite comfortably. A light wooden framework, open towards the front rises above the floor of the 'ekka' against which one can lean; the top of the framework is surmounted by a small domed canopy of cloth, and there are light curtains for the back, and the two sides of the framework, so there is some protection from the sun.

The day before our own departure, we had despatched our own two ekkas to Latamar, and found them awaiting us when we arrived early the next morning. Latamar is not a cheery place at the best of times, but it was particularly melancholy that morning. A sawar (cavalry soldier) belonging to the garrison of the outpost, had just been killed by the kick of a horse, and the village had been quite recently decimated by cholera. 1892 was a bad cholera year in the Punjab, some thousands of natives had died from it in the Bannu district, but there had been only a few cases in cantonments.

We were glad to leave Latamar, and continue our journey; we had intended to stay the night at Banda, but after we had had a late luncheon there, the ekka drivers came and said they would take us straight on to Kohat, as their ponies were quite capable of accomplishing the remaining 32 miles; after some discussion, we consented, and were soon on the move again. We reached Kohat at 8.30 p.m. without any misadventure, except a wetting from a heavy thunder shower. The ponies had brought us 65 miles in 12 ½ hours; they were able to accomplish this distance with the aid of balls, containing some patent equine pick-me-up, which the drivers made them swallow now and again during the journey.

We dined at the Dak Bungalow, and at 10.30 started in a tonga for Klinshalgash, the railway terminus. Arrived there, got into the train and slept. The train started very early in the morning, and in about five and a half hours' time deposited us at Rawal Pindi. Browning started at once for Murree, but I had to go to an English firm, who were the supply agents for Gilgit, and order all manner of stores to be sent after me to Srinagar.

Early in the afternoon I started in a tonga, and passed on the road numerous other tongas full of fugitives from cholera-stricken Murree. I did not care to stay there myself, so I drove straight through to Kohala, where I passed the night.

The next day I drove 93 miles to Rampur, which I did not reach till 8 p.m., so decided to stay the night. Starting at 7 the following morning I soon reached Baramulla, where I found my servants, mare, and baggage awaiting me. My bearer had engaged a boat so no time was lost in beginning the river trip to Srinagar, which I reached the following afternoon, and encamped in the Climar Bagh.

I went over the next morning to the Residency to report myself to the Resident, but he had not yet come down from Gulmarg (a lovely spot in the hills). I went to him for instructions; these did not arrive till the following day; I was directed to proceed to Gilgit and report myself there to the British agent.

I stayed four days at Srinagar, having warm pattu (homespun) clothes made for myself and servants and buying mule trunks, and 'kiltas' for coolie transport. A kilta is like a dirty clothes basket, somewhat bulgy about the centre, and covered with country leather. I also had, according to my instructions, a pair of Gilgit boots made for myself. I have often longed for a pair of these boots in this cold, damp, country, but their appearance would be startling to visitors. They are made of thick pattu, wadded and quilted, and reach above the knee, being secured below it by a strap and buckle. The feet are lined inside with the fir of either kid or lamb. The soles are made of thick slabs of felt, to which are sown additional soles of leather. These boots were the greatest comfort to me, as they kept my feet and legs warm in the coldest weather.

    Encamped in the Climar Bagh was one of the first batch of Gilgit special service officers. His name was Townshend, the same man who defended and surrendered Kut in 1915. I had met him before, as he had served for some time with the 3rd Sikhs, when I was stationed at Kohat. He used to astonish us during the hot weather, for while we all wore the thinnest of white drill garments, made by a 'darzi' (native tailor) he used to appear immaculately got up in what were known as 'Europe clothes' or tweed suits. How he was able to stand such clothing in the hot weather was a marvel. He was a cheery, kind-hearted fellow and could play the banjo, and sing a good song. I bought from him a Double-Barrelled .500 Express rifle, the first sporting rifle I had ever possessed. I thought I could allow myself this extravagance owing to the good pay of my new appointment, and fondly imagined I was going to obtain magnificent markor and ibex heads, as Gilgit is famed for the excellence of this kind of shooting. However, I never once fired that rifle at either markor or ibex; the only animals I ever fired at were a poor old red bear, which I killed, and a fox which I missed.

Having made all my preparations, I started one afternoon for Bandipura on the Wular Lake. This place was distant about 25 miles, and was where the Gilgit road commenced. The construction of this ten feet road had been entrusted to a firm of contractors, Messrs Spedding and Co, and the work had been commenced the previous year. There was not, I believe, a single trained engineer amongst the dozen or so Englishmen who superintended the work of road making; they were just young fellows, who had come out to India in the hope of picking up any sort of employment, but they eventually succeeded in making a good road all the way to Gilgit.

To reach Bandipura, my boat dropped down the Jhelum as far as Wular Lake, then after a paddle of some miles in a northerly direction, we entered a little canal, and reached our destination about 10.30 a.m.

Bandipura was not an inviting spot, and the very reverse of clean. I heard that cholera was still lingering in the village. Cholera had been very prevalent all over the Kashmir valley throughout the previous summer, and there had been a very severe outbreak at Srinagar where there were said to be about 500 deaths per clime during the height of the epidemic.

Shortly after our arrival my bearer exhibited symptoms of what looked like cholera. As Bandipura was the base for Gilgit, there was a large commissariat and transport establishment, and there was doctor in medical charge. I went over to his tent at once and he sent me down a Hospital Assistant to examine my sick servant. I was relieved to hear that he was suffering from malaria and not cholera.

My mare was awaiting me at Bandipura, as she had come in charge of my Sair (groom) across country from Baramulla.

I started my first march for Gilgit at 7 the following morning. My baggage was laden on eight mules, and my sick bearer rode a ninth, so we formed an imposing cavalcade. I had never before had an animal of my own to ride, when marching in Kashmir; it was pleasing to be either able to ride or walk just as I pleased.

For the first five miles, the ascent is gradual, but then the road begins zig-zagging up the side of a steep hill. As we climbed higher and higher I had glorious views of the Kashmir valley and the blue Wular Lake, but all the high hills were veiled in clouds.

The camping ground was at Tragbal (9000 feet) and was situated in a lovely grassy glade in the midst of a pine forest; there was also a good-sized pond, so there was no difficulty in watching the animals.

I started at 7 the next morning. Fortunately, the day was bright and clear and as we were ascending a ridge, I had splendid views in almost every direction; the most auspicious object was the hoary headed Harawitch (16,000 feet) about 20 miles off to the East.

It was a rather stiff spell up the summit of the Tragbal or Rajdiangan Pass (11,500 feet). This did not bear any similitude to the ordinary type of pass, as it was merely the topmost crest of the ridge we had surmounted; for nearly half-a-mile the road ran along a few feet below this crest, and so is exposed to every wind that blows.

Herein lies the great danger during the winter, for a high wind with or without snow would be extremely perilous to any party attempting to cross the pass.

I made a long halt at the top of the pass to refresh myself, and to enjoy the magnificent panorama; as I was doing so I caught sight of a Sahib coming from the Gilgit direction, and dragging a mule behind him. On reaching me, he of course halted and had a chat. I learned that his name was Aylmer, and was very proud to make the acquaintance of a man who had so distinguished himself at Nilt the previous December during the Hunza-Nagar Expedition.

He was an R.E. Officer, and accompanied by a few sappers carrying gun-cotton had made a dash for the Fort gate. He laid his slabs of gun-cotton against the gate, and lit the fuse, and retired behind an angle of the wall to await the explosion. The fuse however went out, so Aylmer ran and relit it, and then again retired to his place of relative safety. The charge of gun-cotton was this time successfully exploded and the gate blown in. Aylmer received three severe wounds, the most troublesome was caused by a bullet which smashed his right-hand rending three fingers quite useless. For this act of gallantry, he was awarded the Victoria Cross and never was a Victoria Cross more nobly won.

He was, when we met, hurrying down to join his company of sappers, which had been ordered to join an expedition against the Black Mountain tribesmen. He had taken four days in covering the 180 miles between Gilgit and the Tragbal, and had ridden transport mules the whole way. He could not halt for more than about 20 minutes as he was due at Bandipura that evening, and his mule was played out.

Curiously enough, Aylmer was destined to twice go to the relief of Townshend. The first occasion was in 1895, when Townshend with five other officers and a force of about 100 Sikhs and 300 Kashmiri infantry were besieged in the Fort of Chitral; Aylmer accompanied the relieving column from India.

Then, when Townshend was besieged in Kut in 1916, Aylmer commanded the force, which had been hurriedly assembled to try and relieve him. Aylmer had no time to properly organise his army, and advanced as far as possible for he had received a message from Townshend that his supplies were almost exhausted. This message was an error, for there were really about a month's supply in hand. Poor Aylmer advanced, attacked the Turks, and as we all know, got badly hammered through no fault of his own.

I have rambled a long way from the Tragbal and must get back again.

The top of the Tragbal is devoid of trees, but after a short descent on the far side, pine trees again make their appearance. The road zig-zagged sharply down to a stream running along the bottom of a thickly wooded valley, and then kept along either one side or the other of the stream. I reached the camping ground at Karakbal at 2.30 p.m., but had to wait a long time for my Sair, as the poor fellow had been attacked by fever on the road.

It would be wearisome to the reader if I gave an account of each day's march, so I will merely give a rough description of the country through which the road passed.

After Karakbal the road pursued its way alongside the stream till the latter joined the Kishanganga river. Up the valley of this river the road now proceeded, passing through the lovely valley of Gurais; this is one of the most attractive valleys in Kashmir; it is well watered by the charming Kishanganga river, and has what is not often seen in these upland valleys, long stretches of beautiful and almost level turf. The hills to the South are covered with dense pine forests, but the hills to the North are only covered with grass. This is a characteristic of all Kashmiri valleys running East and West, and the absence of forests on the northern slopes is explained by the fact that as they face South, the heat of the Sun kills off the young pine shoots as soon as they make their appearance above ground; but I rather doubt this explanation myself and think that the shady northern facing slopes retain the moisture of the melting winter snows, and the rainy season better than the opposite slopes.

Near the village of Gurvais, the road crossed by a wooden bridge to the right bank of the river, and then kept by its side for about two miles, after which it entered the narrow valley of the Burzil stream, proceeding in a Northerly direction and climbing higher and higher.

Three days after crossing the Tragbal I reached the camping ground at Burzil Chuki; this was a cold spot, and in the afternoon, there were some slight falls of snow.

I started the next morning to cross the Burzil Pass (13,500 feet). The road zig-zagged up the bare grassy slope of a steep hill. The zig-zag nature of the road enabled me at times to see my late camping ground, and I noticed that though my baggage was all loaded up my servants and the mule drivers were squatting on the ground enjoying a smoke. I dismounted and halted to see how long they would enjoy themselves, and discovered that they considered themselves entitled to an hour's rest after striking camp and loading up.

The ways of natives are curious; they did not take the trouble to consider the nature of the road for the day's march, and that they would be in my full view as the road began to ascend. They thought that as I was out of camp, it would be quite safe for them to indulge in what is their principle joy in life. This consists in squatting in a circle and passing the stem of a 'hubble-bubble' (hookah) round to one another, while chatting volubly all the time. Their chatter is generally quite harmless, and consists in discussing the price of 'alta' (white meal flour), 'ghi' etc. and the amount of their pay. When the servants and two or more Sahibs are congregated together, they love nothing better than discussing the natures of their respective masters, principally whether they are of a 'hard' or 'soft' disposition.

The Burzil is a wonderfully simple pass, in spite of its attitude, in the summer; but the road by which I ascended was liable to be swept by avalanches in the winter. The summit is fairly level for a considerable distance, and the road ran between what looked like rounded English downs. A most innocent looking place, but very many unfortunate people have perished here when trying to cross the pass in winter, either frozen to death by the icy wind or overwhelmed by snow.

When I crossed there was but little snow on the road, but a good deal was lying in sheltered plains. It was a bright day, and the sun felt hot even at that elevation; his warm beams had thawed the nightly frost-bound road, and made it very muddy in places.

Just as I had met a returning Gilgit officer on the summit of the Tragbal, so on the summit of the Burzil, I met another. This was a very nice young fellow of the name Baird. We had a good long chat before we pursued our different ways.

He had given me rather an exciting piece of news, which was that there was likely to be trouble in Chitral. I must digress to explain the situation there. Chitral had long been ruled by a man of the name of Aman-ul-Mulk; he was absolutely unscrupulous, but of resolute character, and had during his rule absorbed various small states, and consolidated them into his own Kingdom. He lived to quite a good old age, and had died at the end of August. His death was, strange to say, a natural one, for it is the lot of most Mehtars, as the rulers of Chitral are called, to be murdered. He was a much-married man and had left 17 sons. The eldest son, Nizam-ul-Mulk, was at the time of his father's death Governor of Yasin, a small Chitral state not far from Gilgit. The second son Afzul-ul-Mulk happened to be in Chitral, and at once proclaimed himself Mehtar, and began slaughtering his younger brothers, and those whom he thought would be inimical to his cause. Nizam was a man of weak character, and not a warrior, but Baird had told me that he was going to make a bid for the Mehtarship, in which case there was bound to be some fighting.

Baird himself lost his life at Chitral in 1895. The British Agent, Robertson, was holding the Fort there with about 400 men. He heard that the enemy were advancing from the South, so sent out a detachment to carry out a reconnaissance, late in the afternoon. The detachment found the enemy alright, but the latter consisted principally of Pathans, quite a different type of fighting man to the Chitrali, and the detachment got badly defeated; had it not been for the interruption of darkness the whole of Robertson's force would have been annihilated there and then. Baird was mortally wounded early in the engagement when far out on the right Flank; the doctor, Whitchurch, was sent for, and he came with a dhuli and had Baird carried off. Then the Sepoys began to run, and the dhuli bearers accompanied them; a few Ghurkhas stuck to Whitchurch and Baird. Whitchurch lifted Baird and carried him through the darkness, by a circuitous route to the Fort; at times, he had to lay the stricken officer on the ground, while he and the Ghurkhas charged small bodies of the enemy they happened to encounter. The little party at last succeeded in reaching the Fort; just as they were entering, poor Baird received another bullet in the face. He died the following day. For this superb act of gallantry Whitchurch was awarded the Victoria Cross and the Ghurkhas received the Order of Merit, the Indian equivalent of the V.C.

After passing the summit of the Burzil, the road descends sharply for a short distance, but then there is a gradual descent all the way to Chilam, the camping ground; it was a long march [of] 18 miles. There were various snow squalls in the afternoon, and an inch of snow was lying on the ground the next morning; the temperature was 31º, so it must have been very cold on the top of the pass.

The character of the scenery changes greatly after crossing the Burzil; instead of the beautiful green hills on the Kashmir side, the hills were devoid of grass, and of sombre colours, such as umbers, and ochres and dull reds, and are very rocky. Trees too are scarce, and consist principally of the edible pine, and pencil cedar.

I was now descending the valley of the Astir River; about 25 miles from Chilam this valley contracts into a narrow rocky gorge. The engineers were evidently finding this gorge a very tough proposition; one alignment for the road had been commenced and abandoned, and the native labourers were hard at work on another. I had to follow what must have been the original native track, which was very circuitous. Gurikot the camping ground is not far beyond the gorge. A Transport Sergeant was stationed there; he told me that there was small-pox in the village. At this place, I first made the acquaintance of the Kashmir Sepoy; a detachment of what was known as the Body Guard Regiment was halted for the night on its return march to Jammir, the Maharajah of Kashmir's capital. The Regiment was composed of Ghurkhas and Dogias, and the men looked smart and workmanlike.

The road after Gurikot was only completed in places. After about an eight-mile march I reached Astir, the Capital of the tiny state of that name. There was a very good polo ground in Astir, and an ancient Fort, in which was another detachment of the Body Guard. There was a Post Office in the Fort, where I enquired for letters.

Resuming my journey, I passed yet another detachment of the body Guard. It was 17 miles from Gurikot to Harcho, the next camping ground, and my baggage took a very long time in arriving; the 'lambardar' (head-man) of the village took pity on my destitute condition, and gave me some excellent 'chapattis' (thin, flat, unleavened cakes) with which I staved off the pangs of hunger, till such time as my baggage should arrive. Harcho was much above the level of the river, and it was quite warm compared to Chilam, but the road ascended again the next day, winding along the steep slope of the hills.

At Gurais, I had engaged two villagers to help pitch and strike camp, and make themselves generally useful, and they had been imploring me to allow them to return, as the winter was approaching, and they dreaded the Burzil. At a village named Dushkin I managed with great difficulty to get two men to take their places, and the Gurais men departed with great joy.

About half way between Harcho and Duian, the next camping ground, the road passes through a great forest of pine trees situated in a huge bay formed by the hills. I chose a nice spot by a stream for my lunch, and while I was enjoying a smoke after that meal, I descried two Sahibs coming from the Gilgit direction; they proved to be old acquaintances Duncan and Taylor, the latter a fellow 'Piffer,' as members of the Punjab Frontier Force were nicknamed. We had a long talk, and I learned a great deal about life in Gilgit, and also that I was destined for Hunza. They were both in high spirits on leaving Gilgit, and were on their way to Jamma to train the Kashmir I.S. Infantry stationed there.

When I reached Duian, I could see the Indus valley far below; it blew a perfect hurricane that night, and I was barely able to sleep.

On leaving Duian, the road commences descending towards the Indus Valley, and soon enters a terrific gorge. I was much struck with the stupendous cliffs of the Hattu Pir, along the face of which the road had been carved with a fairly easy gradient. This new road was an untold blessing to the coolies and baggage animals working between Kashmir and Gilgit. The old track on the other side of the cliffs was terribly bad in every respect, and was strewn with the bones of baggage animals and even of men, who had lost their lives struggling along it. The track descended 6000 feet in five miles; for this distance, there was not a drop of water procurable, nor was there any shade to be found. It is possible to imagine the sufferings man and beast had to undergo, when climbing up this miserable track in hot weather. Gilgit used to be regarded with the utmost dread by the Kashmir sepoy before the establishment of a British Agency there; pay was rarely issued, food was poor and scarce, and the unfortunate sepoy had, on the march, very frequently to carry his own kit and rations.

At the fork of the descent the road crosses the astir River by a suspension bridge made by Aylmer, who was a most capable engineer, and had built various bridges of the same type in the Gilgit district. The suspending cables were made of various lengths of telegraph wire bound together, and from these cables the roadway was supported at intervals by more telegraph wire.

The Astir River here is an absolutely raging torrent, and it used to be spanned by a rickety country made bridge. In past days, this place was known by the name of 'Shaitan Nara' or 'Devil's Bridge' but a Maharajah had re-named it 'Rani Ghat.'

There was a small guard of Kashmir Infantry stationed at Rani Ghat to protect the bridge. The road onto Bimji, my destination, is practically level, and passes over a wide plain, which is all under cultivation. In 1842 a tremendous fall of rock occurred a few miles further down the Indus, and damned up the river for six months. The Bimji valley was turned into a vast lake, and its villages and cultivated fields were ruined.

The Bimji plain is 4,500 feet above the sea, and though it was the beginning of October, I found it very hot, even riding, and was glad to reach the end of the 18-mile march at 1.30. There was a very nice bungalow for the use of travellers, and I found it pleasant to get under the shelter of a roof again. There was a good-sized fort in which the 4th and 5th Kashmir Infantry were quartered. The Regiments had lately arrived from Jammu, and had suffered much from cholera between Rawal Pindi and Kashmir. The frightful outbreak of cholera at Murree was said to have been caused by their passage through the station.

There was a magnificent view, looking down the Indus valley from Bimji of Nanga Parbat, a mountain over 26,000 feet high; it was a rather distant view as it stood about 30 miles to the South.

Not very long after my arrival at Bimji, a youthful-looking Sahib came in from the Gilgit direction. He introduced himself as Maynard, an engineer at work on the big bridge which was being built over the Indus a few miles further up. I dined with him in the evenings; there was another guest, a man, who though he must have been an ordinary mechanic, had evidently a very good opinion of himself, and spoke of the British Agent, Colonel Durand as 'Durand.'

I resumed my journey the next morning at 7.30, and had not gone about three miles when I came across some ravine deer (a species of gazelle). They halted about 80 yards away, and stared at me. I longed for my rifle, but it was with the baggage.

Eight miles from Bimji I reached the Indus, at the place where the new bridge was being built. There was a great crowd of men at work; all that was, so far visible of the bridge was a partially built pier on the Bimji side.

The river must have been 200 yards wide, but was spanned by a wire suspension bridge, which Aylmer had constructed in a fortnight. This bridge was the admiration of every engineer who had seen it. Before its erection, the Indus had to be crossed by flat bottomed, slab sided ferry boats, which though quite suitable for the placid waters of the Jhelmun and the Wular Lake in Kashmir, were not suitable for the rapid running Indus, especially in hot weather, when the river was swollen by the melting snows. The passage of the river in these boats was a hazardous operation, and there were accidents every year, with considerable loss of life.

The road on the other side of the Indus keeps near the right bank for about a mile, when it turns to the Northwest up the valley of the Gilgit river, which here flows into the Indus. The scenery is not attractive, the hills are bare and rocky, while the lower levels are strewn with stones.

About four miles up the Gilgit river was the camping ground at Dak Parri, a miserable spot. The made track had ceased before reaching Dak Parri, and the old track had to be used; this was so bad on the next march to Minaner, that I had at times to dismount and lead my mare. Minaner was a great improvement on Dak Parri as it boasted of some trees and cultivation.

I had not been there long when two transport officers, Yealding and Minogue arrived; they told me that owing to the approach of winter, all the transport mules would be very soon returning to Kashmir; this was not pleasant news for me as I had left a servant at Bandipura to bring on some of my property, which had not arrived before I left that place. They also told me that Nizam-ul-Mulk had abandoned his intention of fighting his brother for the Mehtarship of Chitral, and had fled with about 200 followers into Gilgit, which he had reached the previous day, and had placed himself under the protection of the British Agent. Yealding and Minogue were on their way to Bimji, and were halting for the night about half-way between Minaner and Dak Parri.

Starting about 8 the following morning I rode straight into Gilgit, the road was fairly good all the way, becoming much better when I entered the cultivated lands of Gilgit. This cultivation extends for five miles or six miles down the valley, and has an average breadth of a mile; all this cultivated land is studded with villages.

On arrival at Gilgit, I reported myself to Major Twigg, the Staff Officer, and he took me up to the Agency – a nice building of the English bungalow type – and introduced me to the Acting British Agent, Mr Robertson. His real title was Surgeon-Major, but since he had become a Political, he had dropped all connection with anything in the shape of medicine and surgery, and had assumed the simple title of Mister. He was a remarkably able and courageous man as well as very determined. Once he had set him mind on a particular line of policy, he pursued that particular line till he had obtained his object, and was not, I think, very scrupulous as to the means he employed to achieve that object. In 1888 he had accompanied Colonel Durand on his first visit to Chitral, which state was bordered by the unknown country of Kapistan. He became imbued with the desire of visiting the country, and did so three years later at very great personal risk. He returned safely just in time to join the expedition against Hunza-Nagar, and when Colonel Durand was wounded at Nilt, he acted as British agent in his place. A few weeks after my introduction to him he engaged in a desperate venture down the Indus valley below Bimji; but what made him really known to fame was his defence of Chitral in 1895, for which he was awarded the K.C.S.J. [Knight Commander of the Order of St John.]

Mr Robertson received me very graciously, and after my interview with him in his office, Twigg took me into a beautifully furnished drawing room (I never expected to see a drawing room in Gilgit) where I read picture papers, while breakfast was being prepared for me. When this meal was ready a servant ushered me into the dining room, which was also beautifully furnished.

After breakfast I went down to the Camp of the Military Officers, who were encamped in what was known as the Bagh. Bagh means garden, but this one was an open plantation of young trees. There were three officers of the detachment of the 15th Sikhs stationed at Gilgit, a doctor, and a Captain Pemberton R.E.; this last officer was only a visitor. Instead of travelling by ordinary route to India he had come from England, via Russia, Siberia, Kashgar, the Pamirs and Hunza.

As soon as my baggage arrived my tent was speedily pitched with the aid of some stalwart Sikhs who O'Brien, Commander of the detachment of the 15th Sikhs, had kindly lent me.

Above and close to the Agency were a row of four comfortable quarters, only two of which were occupied by Twigg and Roberts, the Agency Surgeon.

I speedily discovered that the ordinary Military Officer was not of much account in Gilgit; it seemed extraordinary to me, accustomed to the camaraderie of the Punjab Frontier Force why the Agency Staff and the Military Officers did not all mess together in such a remote spot.

We had our Mess in a hut close to the Bagh; but quarters and a Mess house were being built for the Military Officers at a place called Jutigal, three miles away in the Bimji direction. On the completion of these, there would not be much intercourse between the Politicals and the Military.

I was, according to the custom asked to dine at the Agency Mess, and on the evening of my arrival, had to dig out my evening clothes which I had been instructed to bring. The agency people were very kind hosts, but I was glad when the dinner was over, and I could get away. This dinner was the only occasion on which I wore my evening clothes; it seemed rather a waste of energy dragging them along with me for 500 miles just for one dinner.

Major Twigg told me to stay a few days in Gilgit, before proceeding to Hunza. The day after my arrival Napier, another Political came in, but all the Military Officers except myself were not allowed to come further than Bimji. The reason for their detention was unknown, but it transpired later, when Robertson proceeded down the Indus valley, and captured a place named Chilas.

I remained altogether five days in Gilgit, and enjoyed my short stay very much, the officers being a particularly pleasant lot of men. Our humble Mess broke out one evening, and dined the Agency Mess; the dinner went off very well, but beyond whisky and beer, the only wines we could offer our guests were Kashmir and Ginger wine! I happened to be the Senior Officer in Mess, so had to entertain the great man, Mr Robertson, but he made himself very agreeable. This was the first time the Military had entertained the Agency Mess in the annals of Gilgit. It was rather a daring thing to do, considering the plebeian nature of our liquors, for it was genuinely supposed that when Colonel Durand, the British Agent (then returning from leave) was present, nothing but champagne was drunk by the Agency Staff.

In the garden, where we encamped was the tomb of a traveller named Hayward, who was the first European to enter Yasin, a state about 100 miles to the North West of Gilgit. One evening he suspected treachery, and sat up all night with his rifle between his knees; but he was very tired and towards morning was overcome by sleep. His cowardly foes rushed into his tent and seized him. Hayward asked his captors to allow him to have one last view of the Sun rising and lighting up the wondrous snow peaks. This request was granted. He was lead out at dawn, and when he had feasted his eyes on the wonderful view, he was despatched.

Nizan-ul-Mulk's camp was close to our Bagh, and the whole place swarmed with his rag tag and bobtail retinue, and we were much annoyed by the constant tom-tomming. One afternoon, Suard, the doctor, and I went over to his camp to see a woman dance. A great circle was formed of Chitalis, Gilgits, and Sepoys; Nizam and his higher-class people were seated in a tent. The woman danced in the centre of the circle; she was supposed to have the gift of prophecy, and was apparently inspired by a big tom-tom for after placing her ear next to it for some time, she broke out into a wild song while performing an equally wild dance. We were told that Nizam was consulting her about his future, which at that time looked the very reverse of promising. Nizam saw us in the crowd and invited us into his tent; we accordingly entered, shook hands and sat down to continue viewing the performance, of which we soon wearied. The dance itself was monotonous, and the words of the prophetic song were of course, unintelligible. We took our departure as soon as we could, without offending our host.

    These witches, locally known as Dainyals were looked on with great respect and awe by the natives. They had to undergo various severe tests and perform some horrible rites, such as drinking the blood of a freshly decapitated goat, before they attained to the dignity of becoming a genuine Dainyal.

    I left Gilgit on the 13th October. The mules for my baggage arrived in the early morning, but the drivers were Gilgits, impressed for transport work, and the mule gear rotten, there was a great delay in loading up, and my baggage did not start out until 9.30. I then had breakfast, and started at 11.30 myself. The road crosses almost immediately by one of Aylmer's bridges to the left bank of the Gilgit river, which it follows downstream for about three miles. The Hunza river then joins it, and the road proceeds up the valley of that river. This valley is flanked on either hand by rocky and very forbidding looking mountains.

Soon after entering this huge gorge, I met a gunner, Captain Kaye returning from a shooting trip. He had had an unpleasant experience, for while he was out shooting, his tent had been burnt down owing to the carelessness of his servants. Not long after I parted with Kaye, I caught up with my baggage, so had to go slowly. One wretched mule had already gone down, and smashed most of the fittings of my luncheon basket. The road kept to the right bank of the Hunza river, and was fairly good. I did not reach Nomal 18 miles from Gilgit till 6.30, and the baggage arrived an hour later. At Nomal, there was a good-sized fort, which contained a room for the use of travellers, so I had not to pitch my tent.

Before leaving the next morning at 8.30, I had a look around the Fort; it was an irregular pentagon in shape, with five towers and two bastions, and would require at least one battalion for its proper defence, but its garrison there was only a Company of the Ram Rambir Regiment.

Two miles beyond Nomal a very high 'parri' (precipice overhanging river) had to be surmounted, and there were some smaller ones further on, but the road kept chiefly along the stony valley bottom. Three miles from my destination, Chalt, the road traversed the face of a high perpendicular rock face, and was so narrow that laden animals could not pass, so all loads had to be taken off the mules, and carried across by hand. Fortunately, there were some Kashmiri sappers at work on the road, and were of great assistance, otherwise it would have taken a very long time to get my baggage across. This cliff was the famous Chaichar Parri, which the

Hunza-Nagar people used to regard as the great obstacle to any hostile force attempting to enter their country. Major Biddulph who was the first Englishman to enter Hunza-Nagar in 1876 described this cliff as the worst piece of ground he had ever crossed. Since his time the track had been gradually improved, and in 1890 Colonel Durand had had a narrow road made across the Parri.

Two mules came down not far from Chalt, and on arrival there I found my tea-pot was smashed. There is a fort at Chalt, a square structure of mud and stone, with towers at the angles; its garrison was a Company of the Ram Rambir. I put up in a room in the Fort; it boasted of a square hole in the roof instead of a chimney, but luckily it was not cold enough for a fire.

About a mile's ride the next morning brought me to an Aylmer bridge, by which I crossed to the Left Bank of the Hunza River, and found myself in Nagar territory. After riding another mile or so, the track rounded a mighty spur on my right. When at last I turned the corner, I was almost spell-bound by the wonderful sight, which met my eyes. A few miles to the right front stood the glorious mountains of Rakipushi rising straight up from the river. I have not the gift of describing scenery, so I will copy what Major Biddulph wrote of this view.

"The view of the great Rakipushi mountain from the North side is truly striking. From the water's edge, it rises without a break for 19,000 feet to its topmost peak, which is over 25,000 feet above sea-level. Its lofty sides, girdled with dark pine forest and seamed with glaciers, some of which reach nearly down to the water's edge, overlook numerous fertile settlements, which are nourished by streams flowing from the great mountains. Above the forest extensive fields of snow sparkle and glitter in the summer sun, while overtopping all, great points of granite, on whose steep sides the snow can scarce find a resting place, give emphasis and unity to a scene not easily forgotten."

This description, good as it is, falls far short of the reality.

After rounding the spur the track crosses a strong slope, drops in and out of one or two deep ravines, and these surmount a rounded spur from which I could see the Nilt, where the fighting took place the previous December. The towers of the Nilt Fort had been blown up after the campaign, but the place had been practically renovated; it stands on the edge of a deep, precipitous ravine which our force was unable to cross for 19 days. A brave Dogna sepoy named Nagdu, used to make nightly excursions up the ravine to find a way up the opposite cliff, and at last succeeded in doing so. A hundred men climbed up the cliff led by two British Officers under cover of a terrific fire from our side of the ravine, the top was gained and the enemy's position turned, whereon all the Hunza-Nagar people fled, and the war was concluded.

    I walked up the ravine with two villagers who pointed out to me the exact place where our men had ascended. It was certainly a stiffish climb of between 1000 and 1200 feet, but the whole of it was not precipice, a great part consisted of what was known as stone shoot, i.e. a rotten place from which stones constantly breakaway, and in course of time wear the cliff down to a very steep slope.

Having seen what was to be seen, I returned to the fort, below which the track crosses the ravine, and half-a-mile further on stood the Thol Post. I had been used to the strongposts on the Frontier, and the Thol Post simply horrified me; it was a square enclosure, the walls of which had evidently been made by piling stones one on the other; the walls were too high to fire over, and were very feebly loopholed. The Post could be fired into at short range, and there was no arrangement for the storage of water; the garrison which only consisted of one Native Officer and 34 men of the Ram Ramir, obtained their water from an irrigation channel which could be cut off in a moment.

Not far from the Post was a cylindrical piece of red masonry, evidently very ancient, not more than about 20 feet high. All I could discover about its origin, during my stay in Hunza-Nagar was that it had been erected by some army of Moghals or Mongolians invading India in the dim past.

Thol was only eight miles from Chalt. I had my tent pitched on a nice piece of turf close to the post.

I had not proceeded far the following morning, when I received a note from Captain Younghusband, the Political Officer of Hunza-Nagar, who was travelling to Chalt, telling me that he wished to see me at a village named Ghulmit. Younghusband was the famous traveller, and an exceedingly nice man of the genuine type, and <u>without</u> the Political manner.

I had made his acquaintance the previous April, when passing through Kashmir on leave; he was then the Assistant Resident in Kashmir. The bearer of the note told me that Ghulmit was two miles further on. I had a long wait there as Younghusband did not arrive till 1 o'clock; with him was a cheery young sapper, de Lotbiniere, who was returning to Gilgit.

Younghusband discussed matters with me for an hour, and then we pursued our respective ways. The Nagar villages are very picturesque, being walled and towered, standing in their own cultivated grounds, and surrounded by trees. I passed two other villages, Pisan, and Manapin; between these villages I had to cross a ravine, and while ascending its far side, my mare mistook a long sloping rock jutting out into the path for the path itself, and the impetuous beast dashed up it before I could check her; I managed to wheel her round, and she fortunately succeeded in dropping her forelegs onto the track without coming down. She was unfitted for such tremendous country and I was foolish to have brought her with me.

After passing Manapin the road descends sharply down the river bed, along which it keeps for two miles till below the Tashit Pass. There is a very steep ascent up to this Post, and while riding up it my saddle girths slipped, and it was all I could do to stick on until I reached the top, when I gracefully subsided into the arms of the Subadar commanding the Post who had come out to meet me.

The Tashit Post is on a small plateau, and is immediately commanded by a lofty spur just above it, some little distance off was an Aylmer bridge across the Hunza River, and to protect this bridge, there was a small square breastwork held by 14 men; this breastwork was not only commanded by a very adjacent cliff, but also by the precipitous slopes on the far side of the river gorge, which here is very narrow. The whole position was an absolutely impossible one from a military point of view, and there was an arrangement for storing water. The garrison was one Native Officer and 38 men of the Ram Ramir. There was also a company of Kashmiri Sappers encamped at that time near the Post, who were engaged in making a road on the Hunza side of the river. The distance from Thol to Tashit is 11 miles.

I learned at Tashit that the next march to Aliabad was impracticable for laden animals, and as there happened to be some Balti coolies in the place, I engaged them and some Nagar men to carry my baggage. (Baltistan is a State to the East of Gilgit, and many of its inhabitants were impressed for transport work). I gladly dismissed the Gilgits and their mules, which had succeeded in the short distance between Gilgit and Tashit, in breaking more of my property than had been broken in my trip, during the first half of the summer when I had marched 700 miles.

The Aylmer bridge at Tashit was a frail structure, so the 'sais' led my mare across; the bridge swayed so much that the 'sais' had to grasp the wire side ropes for support. After crossing this bridge, I entered Hunza territory; there was a made road for a short distance, but then we had to diverge on to the ordinary path across the cliffs. I dismounted, and the 'sais' led the mare behind me. The path became more and more difficult, and we reached a great height above the river. The mare was unaccustomed to such bad ground and once or twice quite lost her head. She tried to rush the bad places and once came down, and her hind legs went over the side, fortunately just at that place, there was a slope for a few feet down; the 'sais' hung on nobly to the reins, and the mare regained the path, sweating and snorting with terror; she escaped with only a cut to her near hind fetlock. I was very thankful to get on fairly good ground again without losing my poor animal. I was able to ride on for about two miles, and surmounting a ridge could see the tents of the encampment at Aliabad about one-and-a-half miles off; the ground seemed fairly level on ahead, and I thought my difficulties were over, but after riding for some little distance, I found myself on the edge of a deep and precipitous ravine. The path down was very narrow and steep, so I dismounted and led the mare safely to the bottom; then I had to cross a rickety bridge across a glacier-fed stream, and again congratulated myself that my troubles were over as the path up the opposite side did not look difficult. After ascending some little distance, I came to a very dangerous looking place, as the path for about for about 30 yards was nothing but bare rock with a slight downward slope to the outside. My mare's iron shod hoop slipped on the rock, and she became almost mad with fright, and I came down three separate times, very nearly going over the side, and perhaps taking me with her, but she got across the rock eventually; her legs though were cut to pieces, and quite a large piece of flesh had been torn off the knee of her near fore-leg.

The rest of the path was fairly good, and I got into camp without further incident, but distinctly disgusted: it was hardly a happy termination to my long journey from Bannu.

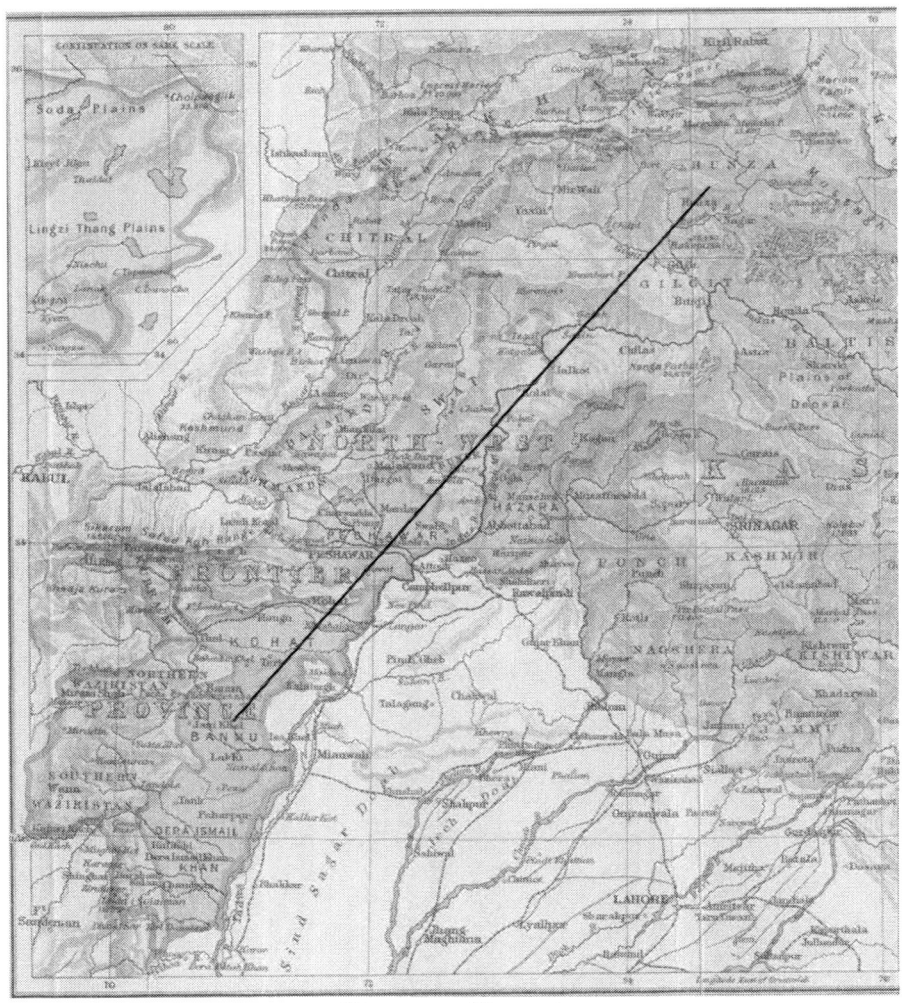

Bannu to Hunza!

Bullet Point Biography of Sir Fenton John Aylmer. 13th Baronet

- **1862:** Born on the 5th of April, at Hastings, Sussex.
- **Education:** Royal Military Academy, Woolwich, London, as a gentleman cadet.
- **1880:** Made a Lieutenant and joined the Royal Engineers.
- **1886-1887:** Served in the Burma expedition.
- **1891:** While assaulting Nilt Fort during the Hunza-Nager campaign, the now Captain Aylmer, blew open the inner gate with gun-cotton that he had placed there and had ignited. He did this while under constant fire. He was severely injured, being shot in the leg and having his hand crushed from falling rock thrown from above. He despatched several of the enemy by firing 19 shots from his pistol as he charged through the gate and fighting hand to hand. He carried on fighting until he fainted from loss of blood and had to be removed from the scene. He was awarded the Victoria cross for this action.
- **1893:** Promoted to Major.
- **1895:** Fought in the Chitral campaign, and was mentioned in despatches. He was made brevet Lieutenant-Colonel.
- **1901:** Promoted to full colonel and made Assistant Quartermaster General of India.
- **1912:** Became Adjutant-General of India after receiving the rank of Major-General.

- **1913:** Married the beautiful Lady Risley, widow of Sir Herbert Risley. Aylmer had a long-running affair with her, which was well known throughout Indian society.
- **1915-1916:** Led the Tigris Corps in the attempted relief of Kut, in Mesopotamia where Major-General Townsend's troops were trapped.
- **1919:** Retired from the British Army.
- **1934:** His wife died on the 18th of July.
- **1935:** Aylmer died, aged 73, on the 3rd of September, at Lingfield Road, Wimbledon, Surrey.

Bullet Point Biography of Harry (Henry) Frederick Whitchurch.

- **1866:** Born on the 22nd of September in Kensington High Street, London. He was the son of a butcher with the birth name of Henry.
- **Education:** Various private schools in England and Europe before studying at St Bartholomew's Hospital in London.
- **1888:** Joined the Indian Army as a Surgeon-Captain.
- **1889-1890:** Served during the unrest along the Indian North-West Frontier.
- **1891:** He became the officiating surgeon for the 24th (Punjab) Regiment of the Bengal Infantry.
- **1895:** During the siege of Chitral Fort, he took a small party to rescue the injured Captain Baird. The Captain was placed on a dooley, but the handlers were either killed or wounded, and were unable to complete the task. Thereby, Whitchurch carried the Captain on his back while under fire the whole time. Captain Baird received another two wounds during this epic rescue, but eventually, Whitchurch and the small remains of the rescue party made it back to the fort. For this Whitchurch was awarded the Victoria Cross. Unfortunately, Captain Baird died of his wounds the next day.
- **1897-1898:** He was twice mentioned in despatches for his bravery along the North-West Frontier.
- **1900:** Promoted to Surgeon-Major. Received two more mentioned in despatches while serving in China.

- **1901:** Was made surgeon of the 1st Gurkha Rifle Regiment at Dharamshala in the Punjab.
- **1907:** Died from enteric fever (typhoid) at Dharamshala aged just 40.

Bullet Point Biography of Sir Charles Vere Ferrers Townshend.

- **1861:** Born on the 21st of February in London. His life started off in a lowly manner, being the son of a railway clerk and an Australian mother. He was though a member of the famous Townshend family and cherished hopes that one day he would inherit the estate, and the title of Marquis because his cousin, the heir, had no children.
- **Education:** The newly established independent Cranleigh School, and the Royal Military Academy, Sandhurst.
- **1881:** Commissioned into the Royal Marine Light Infantry, and quickly built a reputation as being something of a playboy.
- **1884:** Fought at the relief of Khartoum. Here, General Gordon lost his life after refusing to obey orders to evacuate the city.
- **1885:** Fought in the battle of Abu Klea, and killed his first man.
- **1886:** Transferred to the Indian Army, hungry with ambition for promotion.
- **1891:** Fought in the Hunza-Nagar expedition.
- **1895:** Commanded the garrison of the besieged Chitral Fort. His success earned him the order, Companion of the Bath.
- **1898:** Commanded the 12th Sudanese Battalion during the battles of Albara, and Omdurman, which won him the DSO (Distinguished Service Order.) That same year he married his French wife, Alice Cahen d'Anvers.
- **1904:** Promoted to Colonel.

- **1909:** Promoted to Brigadier-General.
- **1911:** Promoted to Major-General.
- **1915:** Townshend found himself in Mesopotamia in the role of protector of the vital oil fields, but he was then ordered to advance his forces and take the area of Baghdad. He was successful in this venture, but decided to rest up at Kut-al-Amara. After a while they moved ahead as far as Ctesiphon, but ended up in a messy and indecisive battle, which resulted in heavy casualties. After this he found himself totally isolated.
- **1916:** As the New Year came in, Townshend and the remains of his 6th (Poona) Regiment retreated to Kut-al-Amara. Here he made an error of judgement. Rather than retiring to the safety of Basra, he decided to make a stand; a siege ensued that lasted five months. Numerous attempts at a relief, including one by Fenton Aylmer, were unsuccessful and Kut finally fell.
- **1916-1918:** Prisoner of War.
- **1919:** Returned to England.
- **1920-1922:** Member of Parliament for The Wrekin.
- **1924:** Died on the 18th of May, aged 63, at Paris, France. His estate came to no more than £119. Or £6,605 at 2017 values.

1897

"SARAGHARI"

Captain Hutchinson's Regiment was the King's Own Borderers (25th Foot), and while attached to the 6th Punjab Infantry was stationed for a time in Kohrit. The incident in this article would have occurred after he had been posted to Hunza in 1892. Therefore, he would probably have returned at some later stage during his time in India and found out more about the event.

Interestingly, seeing that the position at Samana was captured in 1891, he may well have been one of the officers involved in the exercise. This would help to explain his interest and use of the present tense during the opening paragraphs.

🖋 🖋 🖋

"The Government of India have caused this tablet to be erected to the memory of the 21 NCOs and men of the 36th (Sikh) Regiment of Bengal Infantry, whose names are engraved below, as a perpetual record of the heroism shewn by these gallant soldiers who died at their post in the defence of the fort of Saraghari on the 12th September 1897, fighting against overwhelming numbers, thus proving their loyalty and devotion to their Sovereign, the Queen Empress of India, and gloriously maintaining the reputation of the Sikhs, for unflinching courage on the field of battle.

"165 Havildar Ishar Singh etc."

Such is the inscription on the monument standing near Fort Lockhart on the Samana. For the benefit of those who have never heard of Saraghari, or the Samana, it may be explained that the latter is a mountain range, averaging about 6000 feet in height, and running roughly East and West, with its Eastern end situated some 20 miles to the West of Kohrit, a cantonment on the N.W. Frontier of India.

On account of various offences committed by a section of the powerful Orakzai tribe, inhabiting a portion of the Samana, we captured that position in 1891. Forts were erected on various suitable positions along the crest to dominate the tribesmen and to prevent their raiding our territory. The largest of these is Fort Lockhart, the next in point of size being Gulistan, situated five miles to its west, and 1000 feet lower in elevation. Between these forts, rises the rocky, precipitous bluff of Saraghari, interrupting the view from one fort to the other; so in order to establish signalling communications a small fort was erected on the summit of the bluff.

All the forts were rectangular in shape, with two square bastions at opposite angles. The walls and the bastions were about 20 feet high, loopholed only at their tops, and were built of dry masonry, i.e. of stones laid without mortar; the engineers responsible for their construction scoffed at the idea of tribesmen even daring to seriously attack stone walls defended by soldiers armed with breech loading rifles; for the same reason apparently they neglected to provide the bastions with machicoulis galleries (projecting balconies with loopholed floors) the consequence being that if any of the attacking enemy succeeded in reaching an angle between a bastion and a wall of the fort, they would be perfectly safe from the fire of the garrison.

In September 1897, at the time of the almost general rising of the N.W. Frontier tribesmen both Forts Gulistan and Saraghari, contrary to the confident prediction of our engineers were seriously attacked. On the 12th of that month 8000 tribesmen closely invested Gulistan, while another force of 2000 attacked Saraghari. The small garrison of 21 Sikhs made a most gallant defence from 9 a.m. till 4.30 p.m., repelling two desperate assaults, but during the second assault two of the enemy reached an angle between a bastion and the wall, and then with a crowbar removed a few stones; the masonry began to fall, and through the breach thus formed, the enemy in spite of heavy losses, forced their way in, and slaughtered the remnant of the heroic little garrison.

The victorious tribesmen then joined the force investing Gulistan, but it's capture was a much more formidable task than that of Saraghari. The fort possessed the same inherent defects as the one just destroyed, and was further weakened by the existence of a long, narrow enclosure projecting out to the west of the fort, and dignified by the name of a hornwork; this so called hornwork was only protected by a rude breastwork of stones, and was also completely exposed to enfilade fire from higher ground to the West. The garrison though consisted of 160 Sikhs commanded by a very able British Officer, whose wife, newborn child and nurse were in the fort. He had seen the way in which Saraghari had been captured, and took what hurried steps he could to prevent his own fort from being taken in a similar manner.

On the morning of the 13th instant in spite of the garrison's very vigorous defence some 200 of the enemy succeeded in reaching a spot only 20 yards from the S.W. corner of the hornwork, where a steep drop on the slope gave them complete cover from the fire of the defenders. They planted several standards, and were evidently preparing to rush the hornwork, when 17 gallant Sikhs sallied out to attack them. They were received with such a heavy fire that they could make no headway, when 13 more Sikhs scrambled over the breastwork, and the combined parties charged the enemy, and after a desperate conflict succeeded in driving them away, capturing three of their standards, though with a loss of more than half their numbers.

This brilliant sortie considerably dampened the ardour of the besiegers for a time, but there is no doubt that Gulistan would have ultimately shared the fate of Saraghari, had not a relieving column arrived the following day.

When peace was restored, the forts were reconstructed of solid masonry and the bastions were supplied with machicoulis galleries. Levels were also taken, and it was discovered that by raising the existing signalling towers at Fort Lockhart and Gulistan a few feet, it would be possible to signal direct from one fort to the other, so the Saraghari fort was not rebuilt, but a masonry cairn was erected on its site as a memorial of the splendid defence made by the devoted little garrison.

As it was shewn that there had never been any necessity for the existence of a fort at Saraghari, it may be thought that the lives of its noble defenders had been needlessly sacrificed, but it was more than likely that the loss of Saraghari proved to be the salvation of Gulistan. The unexpectedly heavy losses incurred by the tribesmen in the capture of the former deterred them from employing the same rushing tactics in attacking Gulistan; had they assaulted in overwhelming numbers regardless of punishment, it is certain they would have taken the fort before the arrival of the relieving column.

🖋 🖋 🖋

1905-1907

"A BURGLARY THAT FAILED"

We cannot be 100% sure if this experience is autobiographical, but as we have established, the Colonel was attached to the 6th Punjab Infantry Regiment on the Northwest Frontier. Colonel Hutchinson has also indicated elsewhere that he is familiar with the way of the Pathan. It appears that this kind of native activity was commonplace. It is therefore not outside the realms of possibility that at this stage of his career in India something of this nature could have happened.

A final thought. The security system they employed seems very suspect if Kamal could get back into the bungalow for a second visit to leave a vainglorious note.

🙶🙶🙶

There once flourished just across the Indian border, a member of the great Waiziri tribe, by the name of Kamal. He commenced a career of crime by stealing rifles; success in this lucrative occupation led him to the committal of more serious offences, which finally culminated in his heading a gang of fellow ruffians in an attack on the Quarter Guard of a Frontier Cavalry Regiment. The result was the slaughter of nearly every man of the guard, and the capture of the carbines of the slain. In this act of wholesale murder, Kamal was proclaimed an outlaw, and a price being set on his head, he did not again dare to venture into British territory.

When he was a comparative novice in the art of crime, he decided to break into the bungalow of a Colonel commanding a Sikh Regiment, and to relieve him of all the firearms he possessed. At that time Colonels had a small guard over their bungalows, but so far from being deterred by this fact, Kamal considered it to be an advantage, as the Colonel through a sense of security might neglect to take the customary precaution of having a loaded revolver in bed with him.

Pathans always burgle in couples, and on a moonless night, Kamal and his confederate, succeeded in finding their way into the Colonel's bungalow undetected by the security. The confederate then with a drawn dagger in his hand placed himself by the bed of the sleeping Colonel ready to stab him at the least sign of resistance, while Kamal searched for the rifles.

The Colonel was well versed in the ways of Pathan thieves and did not neglect to take a revolver to bed with him; he was moreover, a might sleeper and some little sound made by the burglars awoke him. Lying quite still, he listened, and heard a man's breathing by his bedside. He instantly guessed what was up, and without making any perceptible movement, advanced his hand by minute fractions of an inch at a time until he grasped the weapon, and then equally slowly directed the muzzle towards the sound of the breathing and pressed the trigger.

There was a yell, the clatter of steel on the floor, and the rush of flying feet. The Colonel jumped out of bed, and threw open the door leading into the verandah, when the guard and the servants came tumbling in. A hue and cry was raised, and the bungalow, garden, and immediate neighbourhood were diligently searched, but not a trace of the fugitives was discovered, except a few drops of blood by the Colonel's bedside, and a dagger which the confederate had dropped when startled by the sudden flash and the report of the pistol, as well as by a graze from its bullet.

A few days later, the Colonel found a roughly folded note lying on his writing table. He opened it, and read: 'When next you search for Kamal, do not forget to look on the roof of your house.'

Frontier bungalows have flat roofs, which are reached from the outside by a flight of steps. Up those steps Kamal and his confederate had fled, and lay concealed on the roof until the hue and cry and subsided when they quietly descended and disappeared.

The Colonel and his wife at their home in Orchard Hill, Bideford.

Colonel Hutchinson's and Lilian Byrde's wedding day.

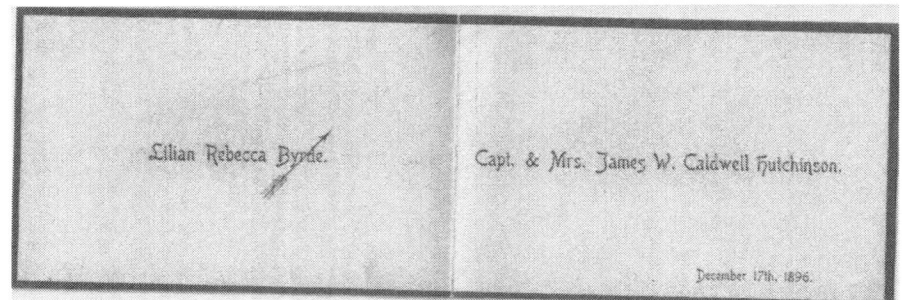

The Colonel's and Lilian's Wedding card

The entrance to Tower House, Orchard Hill, Bideford. (Taken by the Colonel.)

Tower House, Orchard Hill, Bideford, taken by the Colonel, from the garden.

The Colonel's favourite mountain – Rakiposhi.

The Colonel's North-West Frontier Provence.

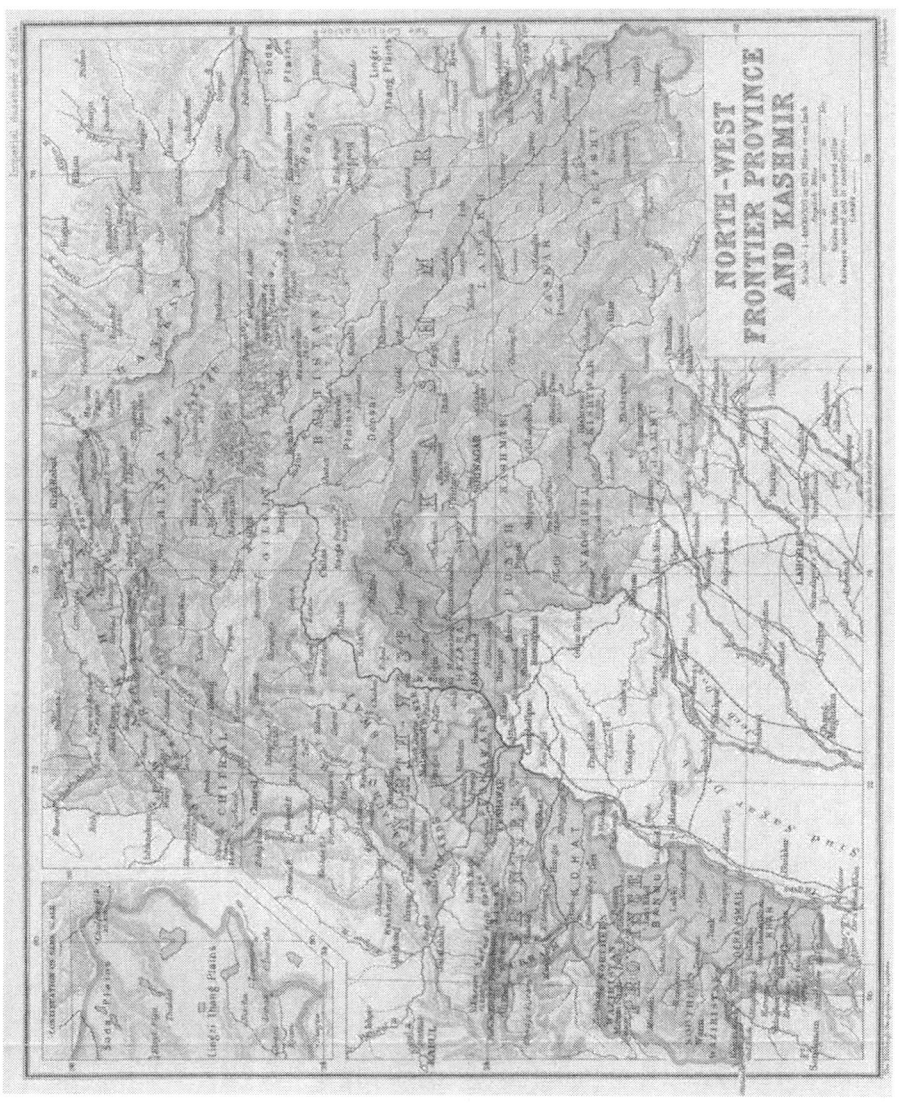

Part 2 – Articles and Observations Made After Retirement.

c. 1927

"TWO EPITAPHS AND SOME INCIDENTS."

With some detective work, the fabric of time can be unravelled to some degree. For example, we can ascertain when these thoughts of the Colonel were written down. In this article, he refers to the "Christianity of 70 years ago." In the context of this article he discusses the Indian Mutiny of 1857. Therefore, if we add 70 years to this date we arrive at 1927. This could be the possible time of writing, just a year before his death.

For some reason the writing style of this memoir is very sentimental and gushing. It could be a hangover from the Victorian and Edwardian days. At that time, men liked their women to be women and tended to be rather mawkish about them. The Colonel certainly was, as can be seen from his feelings for the massacred ladies, and Lady Honoria Lawrence. Of course, Honoria Lawrence's feelings are revealed in her letters to her husband Henry.

Some words are written about the causes of the mutiny. Again, he is slightly at odds with received history. The established thought is that the reason for the rebellion centred around the rumour that some gun cartridges were being greased with cow and pork fat. There is strong circumstantial evidence that this was the case but the fact remains that the native Indian troops would not have used these cartridges and would have applied their own grease anyway. When the agitators discovered that they could not win out with this accusation they began to speculate that the cartridge paper itself was made with fat objectionable to Muslims and Hindus, another invalid accusation. The trouble spiralled from there.

The Colonel talks about his friend Colonel Tonnochy being killed in 1903, but the official Shetland Family History website shows that he died in November 1902 of wounds sustained in the battle described. Another one of the Colonel's little memory lapses.

It is surprising just how small the military contingent was in India at the time of the mutiny. As the Colonel points out, the revolt's failure was due more to a series of fortuitous events, than because of the mightiness of the British Raj.

There is even a light prophetic note from the Colonel's pen. The last paragraph of this article proved to be true because in less than two decades of his writing this piece Britain had lost India to independence.

∂ ∂ ∂

The most interesting cemetery I have ever visited is that of Delhi, for there lie all the gallant soldiers, who lost their lives in the desperate struggle before that city in 1857.

Next in point of interest to me come the little Frontier cemeteries. The cemeteries seem to interest other people besides myself for Winston Churchill in his book, "The Mala Kand Field force of 1897 writes as follows. –

"The passer-by should pause to see the Guide's cemetery, perhaps the only Regimental cemetery in the world. To this last resting place under the palm trees, close to the fields where they have played and the barracks in which they lived have been borne the bodies of successive generations of these wardens of the marches, killed in action across the Frontier line. It is a green and pleasant spot. Nor is there any place in the world, where a soldier might lie in braver company."

The actions, in which the officers who lost their lives, and who now rest in their frontier cemeteries, cannot be described as battles, and many could be described as trifling affairs, but they caused some sacrifice of human life.

I will give an instance of one of these petty affairs, in which a great friend of mine lost his life.

The Kabul Khil, a small section of the great Waiziri tribe had been making themselves obnoxious, so it was determined to punish them.

Early in 1903, two weak columns entered this country from the North, while a third, of which my friend Colonel Tonnochy was the commander entered from the South, starting from Bannu. The column consisted of a few Cavalry, four mountain guns, and about 1000 infantry.

Some two or three miles beyond the border, which is there only three miles distant from Bannu, the columns came across a small Fort, with strong walls built of sun-dried brick, about the toughest material possible against gun-fire. The Fort had to be taken, and the guns opened fire, but made no impression upon the walls. When the attacking infantry got near the Fort, Colonel Tonnochy ordered the guns to advance, and though he should have remained in rear, he advanced with the guns, which again came into action at a range of 80 yards. Even at this short range, the shells had but little effect, and my friend fell mortally wounded. The gate which was protected from gun-fire by a stout wall had to be rushed, and a way forced in. Our casualties in taking that little Fort amounted to one British Officer killed, one British Officer mortally, and one British Officer severely wounded; 25 Native Officers and men also killed and wounded. The garrison of the Fort consisted of ten men. A trifling affair indeed, but the name of Gumati may still be remembered on the Frontier.

This is a world of regrets, and it is one of my regrets that when in India I did not take copies of the epitaphs on the tombs of all officers killed in action, who lied buried in the Frontier cemeteries. When I was first stationed in Kohat I did take copies of two epitaphs which particularly attracted me; of one because the inscription was a wonderful expression of parental love, of the other because of the somewhat quaint style of the wording.

The first epitaph occupied the front and back of a white marble obelisk about ten feet high.

Front Inscription.

Here lies the body of

Ensign W. H. Sitwell. 31st N.I.

Who

Died on the bed of honour

11th February 1850

Aged 21.

Young, handsome, brave, good,

His spirit high

And

Full of hope

Life was before him with

All its

Dreams

But

They vanished at a blow!

Gloriously

Charging the enemy

Sword in hand, he fell

And with him

Havildar Golab Ditchett, Naik Mahdes

Sepoys Meerwa Opedia, and Deo

Band Pandy of the 31st N.I.

These soldiers refused to quit

Their wounded leader

And

All were slain together
Together let their memory be
Honoured
By comrades
Who saw their deeds, and their glory
Raised this tomb
The Officers – 31st N.I.
General Sir Charles Napier. C. in C.

Back Inscription.

We must mourn for him
"According to the measure
that he made us glad."
From the cradle to the tomb
His sweet-tempered spirit, obedience,
Virtue, grace,
Enshrine his dear memory in
His fondly lived and loving home.
Cherished child, thy mourning parents
Weeping o'er thy earthly death,
Transmit to thy distant
But glorious grave
This expression of their profoundest blessing,
Of their undying love
Till that day of joyful reunion

Comes
Through the Redeemer Jesus Christ
Our Lord.
William Hunt Sitwell.
Sara Honoria Sitwell.

The second epitaph was on a solid oblong tomb, and was as follows:

Here rest the remains
Of
Michael Healy
Apothecary
In the Hon^(ble) Co's service
Destroyed by the Afreedies
23rd March 1850

"Michael Healy was an Irishman, high-gifted with talents, energy and ambitious. Foiled in his aim, and weary of his struggle with the world, he ardently sought that repose which he has here found."

Ensign Sitwell lost his life in an expedition against the Adam Khil a section of the very powerful Afridi tribe. Between Peshawar and Kohat, there projects into our territory a strip of mountainous country. These mountains were traversed by a difficult pass, 13 miles long. Known as the Kohat Pass; the Sikhs had paid a subsidy of 6000 Rupees per annum to the Adam Khil for permission to use the pass. When we annexed the Punjab we continued this subsidy, but made the mistake of paying it through a middleman, and the money did not reach the tribesmen; this they resented, as well as an increase in the salt tax. A party of our Sappers, engaged in improving the road through the pass from the Kohat side, were attacked at night and slaughtered. Hence it became necessary to punish the Adam Khil. Sir Colin Campbell (afterwards lord Clyde of mutiny fame) commanded the expedition, and the hardy old veteran, Sir Charles Napier, who happened to be in Peshawar at the time it was starting, insisted on accompanying it, although he was 67 years of age, and Commander-in-Chief in India.

Ensign Sitwell must have been a loveable boy; this is what Sir C. Napier wrote in his journal- "11th February 1850. Four o'clock. Just come back from Kohrit itself, and find that fine lad Ensign Sitwell has been slain during my absence – Alas! Alas! Hilliard too is mortally wounded! These two young men dined with me three days ago, and I took such a fancy for both! especially Sitwell:- never did I meet with a more engaging modest youth. Poor Hilliard talked to me of his young wife! She will soon be a widow now! My God how hateful is war! Yet better to die gloriously as young Sitwell did, than as my dear John did in the agonies of cholera! Fool that I assent to think Sitwell's death best! We know nothing! How can I know anything about it! it was the impulse of a fool to think one death better than another. Prepare to die bravely, and let death come in what form it pleases God to send him."

I have never heard or read of how Michael Healy met his death; it was probably in the same trouble with the Adam Khil, but an apothecary was a very humble individual, and it is unlikely his deeds would have been recorded.

The unusual name of 'Honoria' which Mrs. Sitwell bore reminds me of another 'Honoria' – Honoria Marshall. I lost my heart to her as soon as I made her acquaintance very many years ago; but alas! I never met her in life, and only made her acquaintance in the pages of a book. She became the wife of that great and good man Henry Lawrence.

Major Abbott one of Henry Lawrence's most trusted subordinates has given the following description of Honoria Lawrence.

"Mrs. Lawrence had entered India as a woman, but in her enthusiastic love for him she had come to bless, she found delight in the solitary tent on the sun-parched plain, in the half-furnished comfortless bungalow, in wandering with him through the cheerless jungles, and scarcely less dreary tracts of cultivated land; nothing was without interest in her eyes, and she might perhaps have been less tempted to bless the very wretchedness of these very circumstances which so enlarged her power to administer to his happiness. It was easy to see that Henry Lawrence had found the being best calculated to make him happy – entering into his interests with all her soul, and counting nothing evil that was shared with him.

"She was not beautiful in the ordinary acceptation of the term; but harmony, fervour and intelligence breathed in her expression, emanating from a loving heart, and cultivated mind, a taste chastened and refined, a perfect temper, and aspirations as lofty and holy as those of the noble being to whom she clung."

But perhaps a few extracts from one of her letters to her husband will better describe the woman she was. The letter was written in 1842, when Henry Lawrence was at Jalalabad with what was known as the "Avenging Army" of General Pollock. His brother George was a captive in the hands of the Afghans, and was sent to the English Camp to make overtures to General Pollock. Henry wished to take his place as captive, but to this George would not consent. On hearing of her husband's generous offer, Mrs. Lawrence wrote.

"17th August. And you offered to go in the stead of George, darling! I am glad you did it, and I am glad there was no time to ask me lest my heart should have failed. But had you been taken at your word, though my soul would have been rent, yet I should never have regretted, or wished you had done otherwise…"

"18th August. Yes, you see I did say you were right in offering to go, and further more I shall say you are right if you do go to Kabul. I count my cost in so saying – So do you; and we are of one mind, thank God, in this and other things… God knows while I write this how I could endure the trial, but He has never yet forsaken us, and he will not now."

"19th August. Last night I was a long time awake, and I felt great delight thinking of your offer to your brother, and how pleasing it must be in the sight of our great Redeemer, who gave Himself in the stead of his enemies, that they might be made his friend – even his brothers… The vivid feeling brought to my heart by your love and disinterestedness helped me more feelingly than I ever did before to thank Jesus Christ for what he did for our race, and for each individual of it."

"20th August. And now, my husband, listen to what I say, for it is the steadfast purpose of my heart. You have more than my acquiescence in changing places with George… Therefore, my Henry, if so be it your lot, your wife will be with you. I should be doing my duty, and god would strengthen me in soul and body."

It was no ordinary woman, who penned this letter; her price was indeed "far above rubies."

In the distant days of Honoria Lawrence, there was a great deal of what is known as 'religion' in India, especially in the Punjab.

Kaye in his 'History of the Indian Mutiny' writes –

"The Christian character of the British administration in the Punjab has ever been one of its most distinguished features… Wherever two or three were gathered together, the voice of praise and prayer went up from the white man's tent. It had been so during the Protectorate, when in the wildest regions, and in the most stirring times men like the Lawrences, [?] Taylor, and Hubert Edwards never forgot the Christian Sabbath."

It was well that we had such and similar men during the terrible storm that was to sweep over India in 1857. When we consider the vast extent of India, the immensity of its population, the size of the Native Army (about 250,000 men) it seems an absolute miracle that our countrymen were able to hold their own and avoid utter annihilation, for at the outbreak of the Mutiny there were only 30,000 British troops in the whole of India.

That this small and very much scattered force was able to maintain its ground has been attributed to various special interruptions of Providence, or what a materialist would describe as fortunate accidents. Two of the best known of these I will try and describe.

It is considered that the Mutiny was arranged to commence on one day throughout India; the date chosen was probably the 23rd June; this happened to be the centenary of the Battle of Plassey, and there was a native prophecy to the effect that our rule was to come to an end on that date. If the Mutiny had occurred on one day throughout India, it would have been impossible for our countrymen to have averted defeat, and eventual annihilation.

As it happened 85 troopers of the 3rd Light Cavalry stationed at Meerat refused, towards the end of April, to receive the cartridges which were being issued to them for instructional purposes. These cartridges were not greased, and were the same cartridges that they had always used. A Court Martial comprised of Native Officers tried the 85 troopers and sentenced them to ten years imprisonment.

On 8th May, at a parade of the whole garrison those 85 men were stripped of their uniforms, fettered, and marched off to gaol. This punishment inflicted on their comrades, so inflamed the native troops at Meerat, that they broke out in open and premature mutiny on Sunday 10th May. They timed the outbreak to commence at 6 p.m. when they imagined they would find the entire English garrison, wearing only side-arms, inside the Church, and would be able to shoot them all down. At 6 p.m. the Native Cavalry galloped to the Church but found it empty! Owing to the increasing heat, the hour for Divine service had been postponed to 6.30. The Cavalry rode off, slaughtering every European they came across, and after releasing the prisoners at the gaol, joined the sepoys who had been murdering officers and burning bungalows, and marched off to Delhi which they reached at 8 a.m. next day. A telegraph operator there, succeeded In sending a message regarding the outbreak to Umballa; this message was repeated to all sections in the Punjab. There were 16,000 English troops in the Punjab, and owing to the receipt of this message, men like John Lawrence, Nicholson and Edwardes were able to take instant measures to prevent the spread of the revolt and try to subdue it.

    The message reached the Commander-in-Chief at Simla, and he after ordering the English Regiment in the neighbourhood to march at once for Umballa, hurried down to the place himself, where he collected a small force for the formidable enterprise of re-taking Delhi.

    The message saved our troops from being overwhelmed, but we all know what a desperate struggle it was for them to hold their own in the various districts where mutiny and rebellion were rampant, and whilst ruthless massacres of English men, women, and children occurred in outlying Stations, and in stations where there were no English troops.

I give a rough description of one of these minor massacres. - A party of ladies and officers had escaped from Shahjehanpur after the native garrison had mutinied there on 31st May. They were trying to reach a place of safety, but on the 5th June, were overtaken by a party of sepoys. A Captain Orr whose life as occasionally happened during the mutiny was spared by his men described the scene which occurred as follows –

"When within half-a-mile of Aurangabad, a sepoy rushed forward, and shot poor old Shiels, who was riding my horse. Then the most infernal carnage ever witnessed by man began… Shots were firing in all directions, amid the most fearful yells. The poor ladies all joined in prayers, coolly and undaunted awaiting their fate."

And in that attitude of adoration for their creator, their souls passed into his presence forever.

Splendid English ladies! They shewed the same marvellous fortitude and courage during the three-week siege of Wheeler's miserable entrenchment at Cawnpore, and it is more than likely they did the same during the 19 days they were kept imprisoned by the Nama in the Bibi Ghar, but no lady or child left that dreadful slaughterhouse alive we do not know how they met their fate. There is indirect evidence to shew that they supported themselves by prayer. When Havelock's small army reached Cawnpore only a few hours after the massacre of these poor ladies and children had occurred, there were found in that horrible room, ankle deep in

blood, amongst a litter of portions of women's clothing, tresses, some a yard long, and children's hats, a few books.
Trevelyan writes –

"The list was closed by a Church Service, from which the cover had been stripped, and many pages at the end torn off. Unbound and incomplete; it had fulfilled its mission for it opened itself where, within a crumpled and crimson sprinkled margin, might be read the concise and beautiful supplication of our Litany."

Just about the same time that wonderful prayer was comforting other poor ladies besieged in the residency position at Lucknow. Three ladies and two children were living in a room of which Mrs. Inglis gives the following description in her diary. –

"Our room which really formed part of the native gaol, was a very small, hardly more than a verandah, about 12 feet by six feet with no doors or windows, only arches; but we put up screens and curtains which gave us a certain amount of privacy; and we had an outhouse attached, which we used as a bathroom, a great luxury."

These would be considered confined quarters even in England, but in an Indian hot weather they must have been almost unendurable. Mrs. Inglis was suffering from smallpox. I do not think any of us would like to be shut up with a smallpox patient in a room measuring only 12 feet by six feet, but the two ladies did not fear the risk of infection at all, nor did they think of the heat; they were thinking of the greater danger which awaited them if the mutineers succeeded in breaking through their feeble defences; these defences were so feeble that in one place they only consisted of faggots of wood, over which earth had been hurriedly thrown. When they ladies were able to meet one another at rare intervals, a very frequent subject of conversation was whether it would be right in the eyes of God to take their own lives, in case the mutineers succeeded in forcing an entrance. Some ladies, in fact, always carried on their persons tiny bottles of prussic acid or laudanum.

To return to Mrs. Inglis' diary – The date 1st July, when the enemy made their first general assault on the Residency position –

"Woke early and managed to get some breakfast. John (her husband destined to take command of the garrison the next day, after Sir Henry Lawrence had received his mortal wound) came in and told us, we should soon hear heavy firing; his words were verified, and in a few minutes, the cannonading and musketry fire were most terrific. We felt sure the enemy must get in, where the most terrible death awaited us. We sat trembling, hardly able to breathe, when Mrs. Case proposed reading the Litany, and came with her sister, and knelt down by my bedside; the soothing effect of prayer was marvellous. We felt different beings, and still much alarmed, could talk calmly of our danger, knowing that we were in god's hands, and that without his will not all the fury of the enemy could hurt us. The firing soon slackened, and we heard the enemy had been beaten back on all sides, though they had made vigorous attempts to storm the place."

There was undoubtedly a great deal of Christianity in India 70 and more years ago, but when I first went to the country, very much of it had vanished; at least I can't remember meeting any manifestations of it, beyond the ordinary Church going on Sundays. Even this was looked upon as a bore. There was no Padre at Kohrit, but one used to come over from Peshawar, 40 miles distant to hold Divine service once a month. When the Railway reached Khu Shalgarle only 30 miles away the Padres' used to come from Rawal Pindi, though it was much further off than Peshawar. During one of these monthly visits, in the cold weather too, when all the ladies were in the station, I went to Church in the morning, and found that I constituted the entire congregation. The Padre read the service religiously through to the end, and after pronouncing the Benediction he said –

"I hardly think worthwhile to give you my sermon."

I made myself scarce with the utmost rapidity, feeling very small.

Men went out shooting on Sundays, and acted just as they did on weekdays, except they did not play games of any sort even at mess, as they were all strictly forbidden. One Sunday afternoon I and another youngster found ourselves alone together in the Kohat mess. We exhausted every topic of conversation, got tired of looking at the picture papers and magazines, so we started a game of billiards. We had not been playing long, when we heard a step on the verandah, the door opened and in walked the Officer Commanding the station, a fine officer of the old school. He had heard the click of the balls, while passing the mess, and had entered to find out who were breaking the rules. He went down our throats, as the saying was 'spurs and all,' and gave us the wigging of our lives for desecrating the Sabbath; I felt ready to sink through the floor in shame; my father was a Scotchman, and I have been brought up with very strict ideas regarding Sunday observances.

I think that it was after the death of Queen Victoria that the restrictions concerning playing of games on Sunday was eventually removed. In 1904 I again happened to be stationed in Kohat; the little Church there stands on the edge of the Brigade Parade ground; a large part of this had been turfed for games, and on Sunday evenings while service was being held, the congregation could hear all the sounds attendant on the playing of polo, cricket, football, and hockey. Is it surprising that the natives think we have no religion and despise us accordingly?

There is as we all know, a great deal of unrest in India at the present time, and English people instead of being respected are, I believe, hated. There are of course many reasons contributing to this unpleasant state of affairs, but I feel sure that our complete disregard for our 'beir a din' or 'great day' as Sunday is called by the natives, is one of them.

Quotes from "The Queenslander" Newspaper of Australia in 1902:

INDIAN FRONTIER EXPEDITION.

DEATH OF COLONEL TONNOCHY.
(By Cable Message.)

- **LONDON, November 19.**

In connection with the British expedition which has been despatched against the Waziris and Dharwess Khels, news has been received that Colonel Moraes's column is advancing from Idar, Colonel Pollock's column from Thai, Colonel Radford's from Barganthi, and the fourth, under Colonel Tonnochy, who has been badly wounded, from Gunati. General Egerton is accompanying Pollock's force.

- **LONDON, November 20.**

An official report of the operations of the British expedition on the north-west frontier of India, has been published, which states that General Egerton reached Shlwa on the 18th Instant without encountering any opposition. Spinwan was occupied on the 17th, after some slight opposition by the enemy, and 250 prisoners, with some arms and 3500 cattle were captured. Reuter's correspondent with the expedition reports that Colonel Moraes's column is entrenched at Spinwan. Captain White was killed while at the head of a party from Colonel Tonnochy's column, while storming a strongly defended tower at Gumati. The defenders of the tower, who consisted principally of six tribesmen, who had been outlawed, were killed, while on the British side three officers and eight Sikhs were wounded. Colonel Tonnochy, who was wounded, has since died, from his injuries.

🖋 🖋 🖋

Bullet Point Biography of Sir Henry Montgomery Lawrence

- **1806:** Born on the 28th of June at Matara, Ceylon. (Now known as Sri Lanka.)
- **Education:** The East India College. (Now known as Haileybury College.)
- **1823:** Joined the Bengal Artillery at Calcutta.
- **1824-1826:** Fought in the First Anglo-Burmese War.
- **1833:** After learning Urdu, Hindu, and Persian, he joined the North-West Survey Dept.
- **1837:** Married Honoria Marshall.
- **1839:** Put in charge of Ferozepur in the Punjab.
- **1842:** Fought in the Afghan War.
- **1846:** Made the agent and resident of Lahore.
- **1848:** He received a knighthood.
- **1848-1849:** Fought in the Second Sikh War.
- **1852:** Fell out with his brother John and transferred to Rajputana.
- **1854:** His wife, Honoria died.
- **1856:** He was posted to Oudh.
- **1857:** He was mortally wounded by an exploding shell during the siege of Lucknow during the Indian Mutiny, and died on the 4th of July.

Bullet Point Biography of Sir Charles James Napier

- **1782:** Born August the 10th, London.
- **1812:** Fought in the war against the United States of America.
- **1822-1830:** He was the military resident of Cephalonia on the Ionian Islands, Greece.
- **1839:** He was given military control of northern England where he managed to keep law and order during a time of civil unrest and direct action instigated by the Chartist movement. To his credit, he managed the situation with sensitivity and therefore prevented another Peterloo massacre.
- **1841-1842:** Went to India and joined the Sindh command.
- **1843:** He goaded the untrustworthy rulers of the Sindh into war and brought them into subjection. It is said that he sent a one word message to his superior that used an amusing play on words. The word was "peccari," which is Latin for 'I have sinned,' meaning 'I have Sindh.' For this achievement, Napier received a knighthood.
- **1847:** Napier came home to England.
- **1849:** Napier was back in India as Commander-in-Chief, but by the time he got there the Second Sikh War was over.
- **1851:** Returned to England after a bust up with James Ramsey, the Governor-General.
- **1853:** Died on the 29th of august at Portsmouth, Hampshire. He never married.

"TALES OF A RAMBLER or ECCENTRICITIES"

This article comprises of a number of highly amusing anecdotes, character observations, and eccentricities of life in India. There are also one or two unusual turn-ups. These cameos are very un-politically correct in many ways but they really do convey a strong message about the images drawn.

We can think about the Indian's inability to pronounce English names. One wonders if they deliberately miss-pronounced them in order to engage in some sport with the unfortunate colonials. It goes to show though that it was nothing less than the occupiers deserved because they tortured the Indian language to an even greater degree.

There were some very formidable ladies with strong personalities in situ too. They carried much influence and often pulled rank because of the status of their husbands. And some little girls seem like spoilt brats and show themselves to be 'proper little madams.'

About 2/3rds through the chapter, the Colonel marked a paragraph to be omitted. Why this should be so it is impossible to know, but it does show yet another dominant wife with a submissive husband who carried a senior rank in the army. Just who did rule India?

✍ ✍ ✍

The natives of the Punjab find the correct pronunciation of English surnames – sometimes even of those containing but one syllable – a matter of great difficulty. They pronounce such commonplace names as Brown and Smith, "Broon" and "Ishmit" respectively. The pronunciation of the letter S in combination with a consonant is to them an insuperable stumbling block, and they generally form an extra syllable to get over the difficulty; for example, Dempster becomes "Dempishter," and Gaitskill, "Gaitishkel," but the attractive name of Hastings remains a dissyllable, though it is converted into the repulsive appellation of "Ishtuck."

Natives have a curious habit, when pronouncing names of two syllables, of sometimes reversing the order of the syllables, thus Bainbridge becomes "Bridgebain." I can, at this distance of time, recollect no other instance of such a transposition of syllables except the following, - a smart young officer bearing the aristocratic name of St John, joined a Frontier Mountain Battery; to his horror the men at once dubbed him "Johnson." He was said to have privately instructed the men to pronounce his name, but the lessons were a mere waste of time, for he was always spoken of as "Johnson Sahib."

Natives cannot of course, pronounce correctly names consisting of three syllables, and some of these they make an extraordinary jumble; Codrington becomes "Craiton," Ogilvie, "Ugly," Kirkpatrick, "Krickpit," Arbuthnot, "Buttontot," Younghusband, "Youngassburn" etc.

My own name was a distinct puzzler to the native. When I first joined the 4th Sikhs at Bannu, a fine sepoy asked me my name – those were the good old days when officers and men where on friendly terms – I told him, and he grinned all over with delight, and said that "Hatti Singh" was a regular Sikh name. I realised that he had mistaken what I had said, so pronounced my name again slowly and distinctly; his countenance fell at once, and he made various efforts to get the correct pronunciation, but his best efforts resulted in nothing better than "Huskishim." I was known by this name in my Regiment, but men of the other corps confused my name with "Adjutant." Natives pronounce this word as Ujeetnut," and sometimes prefix an aspirate, and "Hujeetnut" bears some faint resemblance to my name. The Adjutant is a very hard worked officer, and receives many notes in the course of the day; a good many of these found their way to me. This in the cold weather was a matter of no consequence, but in the hot weather when we were to bed about midnight and rose at 4.30 a.m. it was necessary to try and get some sleep during the day, and it was most annoying when enjoying a delicious sleep, to be aroused by the arrival of an urgent note, and then to find it was addressed to the Adjutant.

The Padre at Peshawar, when I was stationed there in 1879, was named Rebsch; the natives converted this name into "Rubbish." Once a month he had to travel to Kohat, 40 miles away to the South to hold services on a Sunday; this necessitated crossing a strip of independent territory by the Kohit Pass. The good man used to consider the journey rather hazardous. As a matter of fact, riding through the Kohit Pass was much less dangerous than a walk in the streets of London at the present time; the tribesmen were in receipt of an annual subsidy from us for the use of their pass, and being like most Frontier tribesmen desperately poor, they valued this subsidy immensely, and it helped to provide food for their families and themselves, and they would not dream of molesting anyone for fear of losing the subsidy, or part of it. When going through the pass one would meet armed men, who might glare truculently and perhaps spit on the ground as they went by, and that was all. Mr Rebsch however felt sure he would be murdered in the Pass someday. Shortly before one of his monthly visits to Kohat he happened to dine at the Artillery Mess, as a guest of one of the officers; during dinner, he descanted on the dangers he would have to encounter when travelling through the Pass; his host though was not sympathetic and observed – "Never mind Padre Sahib if some Afridi does happen to shoot you, we will erect a magnificent monument on the spot where the crime was committed and inscribe on it the legend, "Rubbish shot here."

There were no English speaking natives on the Frontier in my time, so we had no opportunity of hearing our language misused, except in the matter pronunciation of our surnames. Some of us though, did not deal kindly with Hindustani, the language which had to be spoken by all ranks whether English or native. This was not the native tongue of the men we enlisted; the Sikhs spoke Gurmukhi, the other inhabitants of the Punjab, "Punjabi," and the Pathans "Pashtu."

All officers had to pass quite a hard exam in Hindustani, known as the Higher Standard, before joining the Indian Army, but in spite of this, some officers could never speak the language well, and some indeed made ridiculous mistakes. A subaltern 'C' who though he had passed the Higher Standard could hardly be described as a Hindustani expert, was once appointed to act as Station Staff Officer during the absence of the latter on leave. Under the orders of the Station Staff Officer was a Havildar of good conduct and ability, whose principle duty was to see that the Cantonment Regulations were observed by the men of the garrison, and the other inhabitants; he had the power of inflicting small fines on any natives he found breaking the rules.

The Havildar had to attend at the Station Staff Office every day to read out the list of fines he had inflicted the previous day, and the amount was then paid into the Cantonment Fund.

On the first day of 'C's' assumption of office, the Havildar came according to custom, and read out his list of fines to C. as follows: Adam Khan two annas, Muhammad An two annas, Pir Bakhsh 3 annas, Laza Gul 3 annas, Kul Jama 10 annas.

The next day the Havildar read out his list, and Kul Jama again figured at the end. C. came to the conclusion that Kul Jama must be a thoroughly bad character so asked the Havildar who he was. The question seemed to astonish the Havildar, who happened to be a Sikh, and becoming excited he introduced some words of Gurmukhi into his reply of which C. could make nothing.

The following day C. was all impatience to hear whether 'Kul Jama' would again appear as a transgressor of the Cantonment rules, and sure enough for the third time the Havildar concluded his list with 'Kul Jama.' C. banged the table with his fist and ordered the Havildar to bring 'Kul Jama' before the Colonel Commanding the Station on the morrow. The Havildar made a voluble statement which C. could not understand at all, so he repeated his order that 'Kul Jama' must without fail be brought before the Colonel.

When the Colonel came to the office the succeeding day C. told him that he had ordered the Havildar to bring before him a habitual transgressor of the Cantonment rules, and he asked the Colonel to punish him severely. The Colonel agreed, where upon C. went outside, and ordered the Havildar to bring in 'Kul Jama;' he then re-entered the office, and was almost immediately followed by the Havildar who came in by himself. C. at once asked him "where is Kul Jama? Why have you not brought him?" The Havildar ignored these questions, but made an agitated statement to the Colonel, who on it's conclusion looked C. up and down, and observed that passing the Higher Standard had not taught him Hindustani; he gave vent to his feelings by using some rather forcible expressions, and then burst into a roar of laughter; when he had laughed his fill he explained to the mystified C. that 'Kul Jama' was the Hindustani for 'total.' The Colonel repeated the story at Mess with great gusto, and poor C. was unmercifully chaffed about the sinful Kul Jama for many a long day.

If some of the men spoke Hindustani badly, I regret to have to state that ladies spoke it much worse; in fact, they spoke a language of their own, which was generally described as "Mem-Sahib's Hindustani." Their method of speaking this language was to string a number of words together, and utter them without any regard to either grammar or pronunciation; the fair speakers were also not above introducing an English word where they did not know its Hindustani equivalent. The servants seemed to understand them readily, so the ladies regarded themselves as proficients [sic] in the language. The Khansaman (head servant) would listen to his mistresses' daily orders couched in this weird language without moving a muscle of his countenance; he would merely ejaculate at intervals such complementary phrases as, "It is your Highnesses' wish," "Cherisher of the poor," "by the beneficence of your ladyship" etc.

    The only specimen (and a very ancient and well known one it is) I can give of a Mem-Sahib's Hindustani is a sentence uttered by one who was not considered a lady in those distant days; she was a Sergeant's wife who did her own marketing. One day she was attracted by the alluring properties of a sheep's head, displayed in the Bazar [sic], for sale, and asked the butcher its price in the following words – "Kitne baje yik sheep's topi?" The literal translation of these words is – "What o'clock this sheep's hat?" The man though understood her and she got her sheep's head.

    In addition to their eccentric manner of speaking Hindustani certain Frontier ladies were somewhat notorious for eccentricities of a different type.

In my young days, there was a fine regiment stationed at Kohat commanded by a Colonel G, who being the senior Colonel in the place commanded the station as well. The real individual though who commanded both the station and the Regiment was Selina, Colonel G's wife, for she certainly commanded Clem, her husband. Selina was a fine upstanding lady with a very decided will of her own, and a very great idea of her own importance. She liked nothing better than driving round the station with Clem in their dogcart, for as he commanded the garrison all guards turned out and presented arms as they passed. Kohat was close to the Border, so in addition to the ordinary Regimental Guards, there were a number of Station Guards as well. Selina was not only said to have acknowledged the salutes of all these guards when Clem was with her, but she also expected the guards to pay her similar compliments, when he happened to be absent.

Selina was a great stickler for etiquette, and regarded with disfavour any officer who failed to call and pay his respects to her as early as possible after return from leave.

The Adjutancy of a Regiment is much sought after by subalterns, for though the appointment means a great increase of work, it also means a very substantial increase of pay. At the time I am writing of promotion to the various grades went by length of service. A subaltern had to serve 12 years before he was promoted to Captain, and a Captain was not allowed to hold the Adjutancy. In Clem's Regiment the Adjutant was nearing his date for promotion to Captain, and it was thought that a very capable and hard working subaltern was sure to be appointed Adjutant in his place; this subaltern was however rather dilatory in paying his respects to Selina after returning from leave to Kashmir, and the adjutancy was given to another and more junior subaltern. This was certainly an unkind act on Selina's part, but she was kindness itself to any bachelor officer of her Regiment, who became ill; she would have him brought to her bungalow, and do her utmost to nurse him back to health and strength.

I used to know various really amusing stories of Selina's doings, but I can remember only a rather feeble one which I give for what it is worth.

In our Stations, there are no shops, excepting one run by some enterprising native, stocked with indifferent furniture, principally second-hand. Every Regiment in consequence kept a shop of its own, where the ordinary commodities of civilised life, such as stationery, tooth-brushes, soap, hair-pins, collar studs etc could be purchased; but the principle stock of a Regimental shop consisted of wine, spirits, cigars, tobacco, and above all of tinned provisions of every sort and description. It was a great day when a consignment of "Europestores" was received from England, by any Regimental shop, and it was sure to be visited by almost everybody, as soon as the packing cases had been opened, and the stores priced and arranged on the shelves.

With one consignment there arrived a fine Stilton cheese which the Mess Secretary bought for the Garrison Mess, and gave strict orders to the native in charge (known as the Abdar) that none of it was to be sold to any lady in the Station. He had not left the shop long before Selina sailed in; the Abdar had seen her approaching, and knowing her resolute character, hid the Stilton cheese at the back of a shelf. Selina made some purchases and then asked the man if he had any cheese for sale; she received a reply in the negative, but having heard rumours of the arrival of the Stilton, she was determined to have some of it. She ferreted about the shop, and at last discovered the cheese. She ordered the Abdar to produce a large knife, but he explained that the cheese had already been sold to the Garrison Mess. This did not deter Selina from her determination to have a piece of the cheese, and she reiterated the order in her severest tone of voice, reminding the Abdar that she was the wife of the Colonel Commanding the Station. The poor native was extremely anxious to end the interview with the redoubtable lady, and shaking with fear and agitation handed her a knife. Selina cut off a goodly portion of the cheese, and went away with it in triumph.

 Frontier bungalows have flat roofs, and it is the custom to sleep on them when the weather becomes really hot. The roof is a little cooler than the inside of a bungalow, but a 'punkah' is nevertheless a necessity, so each roof is furnished with a stout frame to support a 'punkah.' There was an Irishman known as 'Mac' in my Regiment who had the unfortunate habit of walking in his sleep, so he always went up to his bed on the roof supplied with a stout rope, with which he tied himself to one of the uprights of the punkah frame, to prevent himself from falling off the roof in case he did any sleep walking. 'Mac' went home to his native Isle on a years leave, and on its conclusion rejoined the Regiment at Bannu, the proud possessor of a bride, as Irish, if not more so, than himself. Mrs Mac not only had a delicious brogue, but was a lady of character, and kept George (her husband) in great order.

Just before the commencement of her first hot weather, there was a serious rising of the tribesmen not far from Kohat, and the Regiment had to march at a few hours notice to help in suppressing it. Mrs Mac was, in consequence, left alone for a time, her husband returned after three weeks or so to take command of the Regimental Depot; he could not though get leave to take his wife up to the hills, and she was too new to the country to travel by herself. It became very hot so the Macs were forced to sleep on the roof of their bungalow. Mac, according to custom took a rope up and began tying himself with an air of melancholy resignation to an upright of the 'punkah' frame. Mrs Mac called out – "Now then Garge (as I am afraid she pronounced his name) what are you doing? Drop that rope this minute, and get into bed. If you dare to walk in your sleep, I will give you one across the back with this."

'This' was a thick walking stick, which she had taken to bed with her. Poor George crept very humbly into bed. Whether he dreaded the stick more than the risk of falling off the roof, it is impossible to say, but he never walked in his sleep again. Mrs Mac used to take great pleasure in relating how she had cured George of walking in his sleep.

In my progress through life, I have noticed with some astonishment, that most wives have no objection to discussing in public, the idiosyncrasies and characteristics of their husbands, but I have never heard husbands do the same of their wives.

What the reason for the difference of attitude towards one another in this respect is more than I can say. The only solution to the problem that has occurred to me is that the wife regards her husband as a specimen of the genus 'homo,' and discusses his merits and demerits with other wives in order to assure herself of the true value of the specimen she has secured. (This question has caused me a good many hours of anxious thought, and now that I have the good fortune to be a member of a magazine club, the majority of whose members are ladies, I should be exceedingly grateful to any lady when criticizing this article, if she would be so kind as to give me the key of this perplexing enigma).

Mrs Mac was not only famous for the drastic method she employed in breaking her husband of his sleep-walking habit, but she was still more famous as a lawn tennis player; she was certainly the best lady player I have ever seen, though I admit I have never seen any of the modern lady cracks [sic]. I saw Mrs Mac play at Dera Ghazi Khan the strongest man player in the station, the game was the best of three sets, the man probably thought that he would not have to play more than two sets, but they were set all and he just managed to win the third set. Poor Mrs Mac was rather red and dishevelled after the match, which she most probably would have won, had she not been handicapped by the long skirt of the period.

The wife of one of the Colonels I served under prided herself on her housekeeping and general proficiency in every branch of domestic economy. She regarded all native servants as potential robbers, and had the current market rates at her finger ends in order to assure herself that the 'Khansaman' did not make any overcharge for articles purchased. But there were two very necessary commodities, the expenditure of which was hard to check, these were charcoal and paraffin or kerosene as it was always called in India. I must mention, by the way, that if a group of ladies were seen talking especially together, it would be a very safe guess to make that they were either discussing a rise in the price of charcoal, or the expenditure of kerosene in their respective households.

Charcoal is used for cooking purposes, and I do not know how Mrs M kept a check on its expenditure, but she was certain to have devised some method for preventing any extravagance on the part of the cook in the consumption of this fuel.

Most ladies and certainly all bachelors allowed a servant to do their lamps, but Mrs M always did them with her own fair hands, and the kerosene was kept carefully under lock and key. This would have been considered a sufficient precaution against theft by most people, but Mrs M recognised the probability of the servants abstracting oil from the lamps during the night. To prevent this possibility, Mrs M just before she and her husband were retiring for the night, always told off a servant to collect every lamp in the bungalow, and place them under her bed. She suffered less from inhaling the mingled odours of burnt wick and kerosene for about eight hours on end, than from the dread of having any oil stolen out of the lamps while she was wrapped in slumber.

(When the Regiment changed its quarters, Mrs M with the aid of her servants, was engaged for about a week in thoroughly cleaning up her new home, and the dust was carefully swept out of every room, but as frontier Stations are generally very dusty, it is more than likely that all the dust speedily found its way back again, only it was hidden beneath the matting which forms the home's covering of all rooms. All the doors and windows Mrs M carefully cleaned herself, and it was said that she made her husband join in the task as well. Indian doors are not as a rule made out of solid wood, but the upper are like windows.) Omit.

The Indian fowl is a small bird, and can only produce an egg not much larger than a pigeon. Mrs M despised these tiny eggs and kept English fowls. She spent a hot weather in the minute hill station of Fort Muirro, and took up the English fowls with her from Dera Ghazi Khan. It was remarked that shortly after her arrival, some large eggs in addition to the ordinary country eggs were being sold by the native vendors, who made a daily round of the station to sell what market produce they possessed. As nobody except Mrs M kept English fowls, the large eggs must have come from her poultry yard, but how they were abstracted therefore without the knowledge of the very astute Mrs M has always remained a mystery.

The wife of the Colonel of another Regiment committed many eccentricities, and the idea got about that she was not quite in her right mind, but it was discovered eventually that her eccentricities were due alas! to partaking too freely of the cup that both cheers and inebriates. I have seen this lady come to a dinner party distinctly tipsy, and by the time it was over, she was hopelessly so. A man in that condition is not an edifying spectacle, but a tipsy lady is more than a distressing one. Generally it was very unusual to see a man the worse for liquor, but one cold weather some rowdy young subalterns frequently drank more than was good for them. They were, perhaps unwittingly encouraged by a jovial major, who was fond of an after-dinner sing-song accompanied by a bowl of punch. The morning after one of these jollifications, a cavalry subaltern awoke in a bed, but it was not his own comfortable warm bed, but a flower bed in the mess garden.

  Children were extreme rarities on the Frontier; the famous house-mistress Mrs M had two little girls; the eldest a very pretty child of a sweet disposition, but the youngest was inclined to be excitable and obstreperous, when she became so, she was put to bed, and given a dose of bromide of potassium.

  I once met a charming little girl of seven, she was the daughter of a Cavalry Officer, and was made very much of by everyone. She had a tiny little pony, which she was always riding, and of which she was extremely fond.

  When the weather began to warm up, and the time for departing with her mother up to the hills drew nigh, the child felt very sad at the prospect of parting with her pet, the more so as he would have to be left in the charge of the native groom, because her father was taking leave, and would be accompanying her mother and herself. She resolved though to leave the pony in the charge of one of the officers, and after much thought decided that a certain Captain J would be the most suitable to undertake such a heavy responsibility. She approached him on the subject, and he readily agreed to take charge of the pony.

The day before the departure of the family, Captain J went over to their bungalow and received full and complete instructions about feeding, watering, and exercising the little animal. Captain J promised to follow all the directions faithfully, and to soften the pang of the separation now so near added – "I will if you like teach the pony to play polo." The child drew herself up, and remarked in freezing tones – "There is not the least necessity Captain J for you to try and be funny."

I must close this long rigmarole with a tale of true love.

When I was once stationed at Kohat, there was residing in the place a very elderly widowed lady, Mrs P who had a handsome daughter. There was also in Kohat at the same time, a young subaltern J. who had lately joined an infantry Regiment. This youth possessed various accomplishments, one of which was that he could write the Lord's Prayer on a piece of paper the size of a threepenny bit, but his chief accomplishment was the catching of cobras.

Nothing delighted him more than to hear from a brother officer that there was a cobra living in his garden. He would hurry over to the garden at once armed with a reed pipe, and a heavy bath-towel. On arrival at the garden he was shewn the cobra's hole; he then played airs such as snakes love, till the cobra emerged; he placed the pipe in his pocket and wrapped the bath-towel round his left hand and forearm; this being done to his satisfaction, he advanced towards the cobra with his left arm held well to the front.

The cobra sat up ready to strike, and struck as soon as the towel protected left hand came within reach. While the cobra's fangs were entangled in the towel J shot out his right hand like lightning, and seized the cobra by the neck, and then bore him off in triumph.

On reaching his bungalow he deposited his prize in a 'ghara' i.e. a large and almost spherical earthenware vessel, with a small circular aperture at the top. When the snake was safely in the 'ghara' J closed the orifice with its earthenware lid.

He used to keep two cobras as pets in his bedroom. One night after returning from Mess he found one of the 'ghara' lids on the floor, and that the snake had escaped. Even J with all his fondness for cobras, did not dare to go to bed with one of his lively pets at large in the bungalow; it was the cold weather and all the other doors were closed. J had to search for the cobra with the aid of a lamp, and then catch it, when found, in the manner that I have already described. When he got it back into the 'ghara' he took the precaution of placing some heavy article on the lids of both the 'gharas', to prevent either of his pets escaping again.

I am afraid that the recital of J's various accomplishments has inordinately delayed the tale of true love.

It was noticed that J was a frequent visitor at Mrs P's bungalow, and that D. a very efficient Frontier Police Officer was another frequent visitor.

There was much speculation whether J or D would gain the hand of the fair Miss P. J was the favourite as he was the better match from the matrimonial point of view.

At last to everybody's astonishment it was announced that Miss P had accepted D. J should have shewn a broken heart, but he seemed quite unperturbed. A few days later Kohat society was almost struck dumb when it learnt that J was going to marry Mrs P, a lady more than old enough to be his mother.

Both weddings came off; J's matrimonial venture proved a complete success, but D's did not; in fact after living together for some little time, Mr and Mrs D agreed to live apart.

"EXTRACTS FROM LEAVES FROM A VICEROY'S NOTEBOOK"

by Lord Curzon

The mountain of Rakipushi deeply affected Colonel Hutchinson as we have observed already. It also affected one of India's Viceroys, Lord Curzon. The Colonel must have come across this piece of writing one day, and because it struck a chord with him, decided to reproduce it.

The Colonel's writing of this narrative leaves much to be desired. As a result, some of the words are unintelligible. These are entered as [?] in the text, but it does not badly affect the reading.

Again, it is very gushing, with a strong and articulate, vocabulary. But then why not? He is another Victorian!

🖋 🖋 🖋

In the Hunza valley and its immediate environs, within a radius of about 50 miles of its Capital, Baltit, are congregated some of the most striking physical phenomena in the universe. Here a tumult of the highest known mountains lift thin unscaled peaks above the deepest valleys, the most sombre ravines. Within a range of 70 miles there are eight crests with an elevation of over 24,000 feet, while the little state of Hunza alone is said to contain more summits of over

20,000 feet than there are of over 10,000 feet in the entire Alps. The largest glaciers on the globe outside of the Arctic Circle pour their frozen cataracts down the rivers and contoured hollows of the mountains. Great rivers foam and thunder in flood time along the resounding gorges, though sometimes reduced in winter – the season of low waters – to [?] the [?]. Avalanches of snow, and still more remarkable – of mud, come plunging down the long slopes, and distort the face of nature as though by some lamentable disease. In the valley of the Hunza river up which my track lay, nature would seem to have exerted her supreme energy, and in one chord to have composed almost every note in her vast and majestic diapason of sound. For there she shews herself in the same moment both tender and savage, both radiant and appalling, the relentless spirit that hovers above the ice-towers and the gentle pastures of the field and orchard, the tutelary deity of the haunts of man.

 Never can I forget the abruptness and splendour of the surprise when, shortly after leaving the fort of Chalt, 30 miles beyond Gilgit, there soared into view the lovely apparition of the great mountain Rakipushi, lifting above the bolder strewn and forest clad [?] of his lower stature 18,000 feet of unsullied ice and snow to a total height of 25,500 feet above the sea. Next to the sight of Kanchenjunga from beyond Darjeeling, this is the finest mountain spectacle that I have seen. Rakipushi is one of the most superbly modelled of mountains. Everywhere visible as we ascend the valley, he keeps watch over the lower summits, and over the smiling belts of green, and the orchard plots below that owe their existence to his glacial bounty. But up above, where no raiment but the royal ermine clothes his shoulders, his true majesty is best revealed. There enormous and shining glaciers fill the hollows of his sides, the ice-fields stretch for mile after mile of breadth and height, and only upon the needle point of his highest crest is the snow unable to settle. In that remote empyrean we visualise an age beyond the boundaries of human thought, a silence as from the dawn of time. And though the eye, aching with the dazzling vision, may seek a transient solace in the restful verdure of the lower and terraced slopes, may wander over the cultivated surface of the alluvial farms, and may even dip into the deep gorge where the river hums 1000 feet below our feet yet it cannot for long resist the enchantment of those glimmering peaks, and ever hankers for the fascination of the summit. Rakipushi stands there, and will stand as long as this orb endures, under the heavenly vault, under the eternal stars, [?], godlike, sublime, tremendous.

Bullet Point Biography of George Nathanial Curzon, 1ˢᵗ Marquis of Kedleston

- **1859:** Born on the 11ᵗʰ of January at Kedleston, Derbyshire.
- **Education:** Wixenford School. Eton College, and Balliol College, Oxford.
- **1885:** Assistant Private Secretary to Lord Salisbury.
- **1886:** Elected MP for Southport, Lancashire.
- **1891-1892:** Under-Secretary of State for India.
- **1895:** Married Mary Leitner, the daughter of an American millionaire department store owner.
- **1895-1898:** Under-Secretary of State for Foreign Affairs.
- **1899:** Made Viceroy of India and was created Baron Curzon of Kedleston.
- **1905:** Returned to Britain.
- **1906:** His wife Mary died aged 36.
- **1907:** Elected Chancellor of Oxford University.
- **1908:** Made a Lord, meaning that he could not return to the House of Commons even if he wanted to.
- **1911:** Created Baron Ravensdale of Ravensdale, Derbyshire.
- **1915:** joined the coalition government as Lord Privy Seal.
- **1916:** Served as Leader of the House of Lords.
- **1917:** Married his second wife, Grace Hinds, another wealthy American widow.
- **1919-1924:** Foreign Secretary.

- **1925:** Died on the 20th of March from a bladder haemorrhage aged 66, and was buried in the family vault at All Saints church, near the family home of Kedleston Hall.
- **1958:** The death of his wife Grace on the 29th of June.

"NATIVE PETITION."

Whether this is the genuine article, or something made up by Colonel Hutchinson and/or his friends we will never know. All the same, it's a magnificent play on words and it's a bit of fun, revealing again that the stuffy old Colonel had a sense of humour. It's politically incorrect of course, but there is no malice behind it, and it should really be taken in the spirit it is given. This is a job application and C.V. British Raj in India style.

∂ ∂ ∂

Respectfully sheweth. That your honour's servant is poor man in agricultural behaviour and much depends on season for staff of life, therefore he prays that you will favour upon him and take him into your Saintly service that he may have some permanently labour for the support of his soul and his family; wherefore he falls on his family's bended knees and implores you of this merciful consideration to a wretched miserable like your honour's unfortunate petitioner. That your lordship's honour's servant was too much poorly during the last rains and was resuscitated by much medicines which made magnificent excavations in the coffers of your honourable servant whose means are circumcised by his large family consisting of five female women and three masculine, the last of which are still taking milk from mother's chest and are horribly noiseful through pulmonary catastrophe in their interior abdomen. That your honour's miserable servant was officiating in several capabilities in past generations but has become too much old for espousing hard labour in this time of his bodily life, but was not drunked, nor thief, nor swindler, nor any of these kind, but was always pious and affectionate to his numerous family consisting of the aforesaid five female women and three males, the last of whom are still milking their parental mother. That your generous honour's lordship's servant was entreating magistrate for employment in municipality to receive filth etc. but was not granted petition. Therefore your generous lordship will give me some easy cook in the department or something of this sort. For which act of kindness, your noble lordship's poor servant, will as in duty bound, pray for your longevity and procreativeness.

"LIFE HISTORY OF KATE AND REVERSALS"

Here is a bit of fun. It may seem rather tame to modern generations who have their televisions, videos, computer games, music CDs, the Internet, and other untold diversions. But, one thought as to the setting for this brings it all into context. When the colonel was stationed in the wilds of India, there were none of these things, not even when he was at home. To use an old cliché, he had to make his own entertainment. He was an intelligent and well-educated man as is shown by his desire to write articles, keep diaries, and record journals. So, it should come as no surprise to find that he entertained himself with word games on those long, lonely evenings. This ties in with the Victorian ethic of profitable activity that educates and stimulates rather than the modern ethic that dumbs-down and stupefies. His detailed educational history is not known but as we've seen he attended a private school in Bristol, and then a military establishment in York.

These are good games for family and friends to play at get-togethers. One person could ask the questions and the rest of the party could try to supply the answer. This is more mentally stimulating than television. Why not try and think up your own?

"KATE"

Answers:

1) She has a double. — Duplicate.

2) She chews her food properly. — Masticate.

3) She inscribes her poems to a friend. — Dedicate.

4) She tries to please. — Placate.

5) She is very pale. — Delicate.

6) She tells where she lives. — Locate.

7) She tries to teach the young. — Educate.

8) She pulls out her shoulder. — Dislocate.

9) She reasons unsoundly. — Sophisticate.

10) She pronounces judgement on another. — Adjudicate.

11) She is oppressed and chokes. — Suffocate.

12) She becomes assertive. — Predicate.

13) She foretells coming events. — Prognosticate.

14) She resigns a good office. — Abdicate.

15) She tries to escape from perplexities. — Extricate.

16) She becomes oily and smooth textured. — Lubricate.

17) She dissembles with the truth. — Prevaricate.

18) She becomes vulgar and unrefined. — Indelicate.

19) She returns kindness with kindness.   Reciprocate.

20) She is expelled from college.   Rusticate.

21) She is most difficult to deal with.   Intricate.

22) She gets another into trouble.   Implicate.

23) She becomes very regretful.   Deprecate.

24) She asks for alms.   Supplicate.

25) She becomes a thief.   Confiscate.

26) She pleads in a court of justice.   Advocate.

27) She defends herself.   Vindicate.

28) She tries to efface her identity.   Eradicate.

29) And becomes one of a public company.   Syndicate.

"REVERSALS"

1) A puddle reversed becomes a noose.

    Pool – Loop.

2) A black substance is converted into a rodent.

    Tar – Rat.

3) A useful receptacle is changed into a prize.

    Drawer – Reward.

4) A snare is turned into a sub-division.

    Trap – Part.

5) To have life becomes wickedness.

    Live – Evil.

6) A china utensil becomes a child's toy.

    Pot – Top.

7) Attire becomes a hateful boast.

    Garb – Brag.

8) A domestic pet becomes an idol.

    Dog – God.

9) An instrument changes to the spoils of war.

    Tool – Loot.

10) An oriental potentate is converted into a frost.

    Emir – Rime.

11) The peak of a hill turned into distemper.

    Tor – Rot.

12) Conflict and battle become uncooked articles.

    War – Raw.

13) This provides an exit and changes into a measure.

    Door – Rood.

14) I have a terrible disease and when reversed causes repulsion.

    Leper – repel.

15) Blossoms of the hedge turn into a root.

    May – Yam.

16) An oriental native becomes an apartment.

    Emir – Rime.

17) An outdoor game changes into a schoolboy's punishment.

    Golf – Flog.

18) An Irish name is changed into a light blow.

    Pat – Tap.

19) Part of a verb becomes a pronounced sentence.

    Mood – Doom.

20) A public school is changed to importance.

    Eton – Note.

21) A deep abyss changes to a visitors gift.

    Pit – Tip.

22) Bereft of reason when reversed becomes a sheep.

    Mad – Ram.

23) A pet dog is turned into a kitchen requisite.

    Pom – Mop.

24) A hospital room becomes a tie in games.

    Ward – Draw.

25) A fastener changes into a pinch.

    Pin – Nip.

26) The flap of a garment is turned into a friend.

    Lap – Pal.

27) A Scottish dance is turned into a sly look.

    Reel – Leer.

28) A freshwater fish becomes connected with the wind.

    Eel – Lee.

29) A dessert fruit is changed into a barrel.

    Nut – Tun.

30) A receptacle for wine changes into the point of a pen.

    Bin – Nib.

31) A fisherman's requisite becomes a numeral.

    Net – Ten.

32) A short snooze turns into a cooking utensil.

    Nap – Pan.

Part 3 – His Final Word and His Reader's Comments.

"BATHOS"

This entry in the Colonel's Notebook is an interesting contrast to the rest. The Colonel converts one of his experiences into a short story, with Colonel Smith being a thinly disguised alias for Colonel Hutchinson himself.

The experience probably happened shortly after the Colonel retired from the Indian army and was invalided back to England. He was living at a place called Southcott House in the village of Weare Gifford, which nestles snugly on the banks of the River Torridge in North Devon. It is plainly discernible that the Colonel fits into the position of George Orwell's upper-middle class, as mentioned in the introduction.

The commanding presence of Mount Rakipushi certainly made a lasting impression upon the Colonel because in the notebook he includes the experiences of others who have been moved by the sight. Colonel Hutchinson produced a painting of Rakipushi in 1898, but unfortunately it has faded badly.

🖉 🖉 🖉

Colonel Smith after many years service in India, retired to England, and settled down in a country village. He was exceedingly fond of shooting, but realised the fact that his modest pension would not permit any indulgence in his favourite sport. His neighbours apparently took it for granted that he was no sportsman, as he did not hunt, shoot, or fish, and though he admitted that he had done a considerable amount of shooting, not one of them evinced the slightest interest in Indian sport; they preferred to expatiate on their own performances in hunting, shooting, and fishing, all of which they could obtain within a radius of a few miles from the front doors of their comfortable homes.

Colonel Smith had travelled hundreds of miles from the nearest railway to reach his shooting ground in the vicinity of some of the world's highest mountains, and had been fortunate enough to spend an enjoyable year on duty in the Gilgit district. He retained an enthusiastic admiration for the mighty ice peaks he had lived amongst, so once when entertaining a sporting neighbour, and becoming rather bored by the endless recitation of the slaughter, of pheasants, rabbits etc, he thought he would change the conversation by attempting to describe some of the mountain scenery he knew and loved so well.

One view in particular had left a vivid impression on his memory. When stationed in Hunza, he obtained a few days leave to shoot Markhor on one of the lower slopes of Rakipushi, a giant of 25,500 feet. While climbing this spur he found himself on the edge of a precipitous drop facing the main mass of the mountain; he was just below the snowline, so he calculated his elevation at that season of the year to be about 12,000 feet. From his standing point he could look down 10,000 feet to the valley of the Hunza River (10,000 feet above sea level) and then lifting his gaze up the mountain's sides, found it finally resting on the sharp peak which cleft the unclouded sky 13,500 feet above his head.

The sudden view of this glorious mountain, one vast uplifted sheet of glittering ice and snow, it's dazzling purity only broken here and there by projecting rock, and by the deep blue and green sides of the hanging glaciers, the whole crowned by the triangular rock face of the summit, so near in point of actual distance, but as regards accessibility as remote as the North Pole, almost took his breath away.

This was the marvellous view he thought he would attempt to describe to his garrulous acquaintance, but he had scarcely commenced his description when his guest interrupted him by exclaiming – "Oh! I have seen something wonderful too. One day when out fishing, I saw seven young Kingfishers, all sitting in a row on the same branch."

Poor Colonel Smith, a modest and retiring individual felt distinctly suppressed, and never again dared to speak of his Indian experiences to any of his sporting acquaintances.

"CRITICISMS – 1"

"Two Epitaphs etc."

This is a collection of observations and comments surrounding the "Two Epitaphs" article by the Colonel's friends, colleagues, and I would imagine, the editorial board of the Amateur Magazine, he wished to write for.

Many of the sentiments expressed by the commentators hold good for today. Indeed, Britain has become an even more secular society than it was in the 1920s. By contrast, since the 1950s, the large immigrant population have brought with them a stronger, and more devoted religious base. Whilst Christendom has shrivelled and withered on the tree Islam has gone into the ascendancy, even in this country, with many converts coming from 'Christianity.' Time has shown that materialism is not the answer, and the established church has sold its soul to the Devil, so the spiritual vacuum must be filled. If it were feasible that this old system went on for another 200 years, then the probability is that Britain would be a Muslim country with Christendom a very minor religion; the second largest religion being no doubt, atheistic materialism.

Finally, of course, how true it is that today's children, and the majority of today's adults (who are yesterday's children) do worship the 'Goddess Pleasure.'

Very interesting reminiscences. "Prepare to die bravely and let death come in what form it pleases God to send him" is a noble and inspiring saying. Honoria Lawrence, whom I meet here for the first time, is a fine woman worthy of the best traditions of our race. Some of J.W. H's concluding remarks borne out by what I know of east Africa, and of which I hope to write more someday.

    E. Le N. F.

A most interesting article in many ways, and trust that J.W. H will give us more such.

    A.G.H.

Interesting, as are all J.W. H's Indian memories.

    M.G.P.

Very interesting.

    D.C.

A very splendid article.

    E.B.T.

A perfectly fascinating article on a subject that thrills one. I <u>quite</u> agree with the concluding lines of the article.

K.S.

A splendid and inspiring article, admirably written. The carelessness of many English people about the observances of their religion must be very shocking to devout Hindus and Mohammedans.

E.L.W.

Splendid article, well written. Yes, when England was simpler and observed her religious duties, she was prosperous and respected by all. Now that she devotes her Sundays to motoring, and is rivalling the United States in her Divorce Cases, she no longer holds the high position she once did. Her young people are growing up as worshippers of the Goddess Pleasure! We may well learn a lesson from those who died so bravely in the Indian Mutiny.

P. McM.

"CRITICISMS –2"

"Bannu to Hunza Pt1."

These criticisms are for the Bannu to Hunza travelogue, which as can be seen by the commentaries, were originally written as two articles. Two of the contributors suggest that the Colonel bring these articles out in book form. This never happened in his lifetime, but now his wish has been fulfilled, which is a fitting conclusion to this unique collection of personal memories from the days of the British Raj in India.

Finally, the endnote by Colonel Hutchinson is light-hearted, and so the Colonel's Notebook ends with an exclamation of surprise and amusement. As many of the commentators confirm, he has his own interesting style. This reinforces the fact that as often as not, it ain't what you say, it's the way that you say it!

Most interestingly written.

D.C

Interesting as usual.

E.L.N.F.

Splendidly told.

K.S.

A well written article. I think Colonel H ought to bring these articles out in book form, and so give pleasure to a wider public.

P.McM.

P. McM's idea is excellent for J.W.H has an entertaining and informing style all his own.

A.E.T.D.

Very interesting and well written.

M.G.P.

These articles are always interesting; this is not less so than its predecessors.

E.B.T.

"Bannu to Hunza Pt2"

Most descriptive and intensely interesting, and to me the details about the mare are especially interesting.

E.B.T.

Very interesting.

D.C.

Splendid.

    K.S.

J.W.H has a wonderful memory to recall all the details. Good reading.

    A.E.H.

Delightful as are all J.W.H's Indian reminiscences.

    M.G.P.

Most interesting. I think J.W.H ought to collect his reminiscences into book form.

    P.M^cM.

J.W.H is interesting here as usual. I hope he will give us many more such articles.

    E.Le.N.F.

    (End note by J.W.C.H.)

This article did not interest the readers of the A.M. and it only obtained five votes, the same number obtained by a lady who described a ride in a bath chair at Brighton! Her article covered four pages of foolscap, and mine covered 16!

ENDS

A Short Glossary

A.M.: Amateur Magazine.

Anglo-Indian: Citizens of mixed race resulting from British and Indian marital relationships. Generally thought of as inferior types.

Anna: 1 sixteenth of a rupee.

Bagh: A garden. E.g. Climar Bagh.

Brevet: A warrant that gives a commissioned officer the title of a higher rank as a reward for bravery or some other praiseworthy activity, although the recipient has not the authority, and doesn't receive the pay of the real rank. Therefore, the honour holds no real worth except for a bit of ego-boosting swank.

Brigade: An army unit comprising, infantry, cavalry, and artillery. Usually led by a Brigadier.

Bungalow: A single storied residence in the country.

Cantonment: (Pronounced cantoonment.) A governmental department area.

Cape Camorin: The southernmost tip of the Indian continent.

C.B.: Companion of the Order of the Bath.

Char: Tea. Hence the common expression, a cup of char.

Cheroot: A small cigarette sized cigar.

Cholera: An infectious disease that causes diarrhoea and vomiting.

Clime: A region.

Collector: For all intents and purposes, the tax collector. Usually the chief administrator of a district.

Coolie: An unskilled Indian labourer.

Dak: Mail. Hence, a dak bungalow is a government staging post or post office.

Dhuli: A form of Indian bed or stretcher.

District: An Indian area of administration.

Division: A collection of army brigades and regiments.

Dysentery: An intestinal inflammation causing extreme diarrhoea.

Ekka: A small, two wheeled cart pulled by a pony.

Ensign: The lowest ranked commissioned infantry officer.

G.C.B.: Knight Grand Cross of the Order of the Bath.

Ghari: A large horse-drawn cart.

Ghi: Clarified Indian butter.

Gymkhana: A sporting event. (Not just to do with horses.)

Half-Mounting: The sepoys of the Indian army had to pay the cost of their ordinary fatigue dress from a small allowance provided.

Havildar: An Indian non-commissioned officer. Roughly the equivalent of a sergeant in the British army.

Hill Station: Premises built above 5000 feet. This is where the central, and state, governments moved to during the "hot weather."

Jezail: A long-barrelled musket, a favourite weapon of the Pathans.

K.C.B.: Knight Commander of the Order of the Bath.

K.C.S.J.: A medal. A Roman Catholic honour. Knight Commander of the Order of Saint John. It does not come with a national knighthood, and carried no formal title.

Laudanum: A painkiller based on morphine.

Markor: An Indian antelope.

Memsahib: A lady.

Mussulman: A Muslim.

Naik: The Indian army equivalent of the British army corporal.

Pathan: Pushtu speaking Muslims living on the North-Western Frontier and southern parts of Afghanistan.

PIFFERS: Members of the Punjab Frontier Force.

Pith Helmet: A lightweight hat (topee) made from plant fibres.

Prussic acid: Hydrocyanic acid. A strong poison.

Punkah: Before the days of electricity, this was a hand operated swinging fan suspended from a frame.

Quarter-guard: A military detachment guarding the living quarters.

Rakaposhi: (Rakipushi.) This mountain is unique as it is the only mountain that goes straight up from cultivated agricultural land to a height of 25,551 feet. This incredible sight can be seen right from the bottom to the top in certain places.

Raj: A kingdom. Often used to denote Britain's rule in India.

Regiment: A large unit of soldiers led by a Colonel.

Rupee: The chief currency unit of India. It was worth roughly two shillings (ten pence) in 1857.

Sahib: Sir, master, or lord. A mark of respect, addressed by Indians to Europeans.

Sapper: The official term for a private solder in the Royal Engineers.

Sepoy: A native Indian with the rank of private under British command.

Sikh: A religion founded in the 15th century by unhappy Hindus.

Sowar: Indian cavalry trooper of other rank status.

Subadar: An Indian Lieutenant in the army of the East India Company.

Tonga: A light, two wheeled, horse-drawn carriage.

Tommy (Thomas) Atkins: The ordinary British soldier of other rank status. From the specimen name used on army forms.

Urdu: The language of northern India. A more complex form of Hindustani.

Viceroy: The chief office of rulership in a foreign colony. The monarch's proxy ruler.

Further Reading

Keay, John, *India, a History*, (2000)

David, Saul, *The Indian Mutiny 1857*, (2002)

Ed. Allen, Charles, *Plain Tales From the Raj*, (1976)

James, Lawrence, *Raj, the Making and the Unmaking of British India*, (1997)

Collingham, E.M., *Imperial bodies*, (2001)

Battye, Evelyn, and Elgee, Cecil, *Costumes and Characters of the British Raj*, (1982)

Judd, Denis, *The British Raj*, (1972)

Edwardes, Michael, *Raj*, (1967)

Hello everyone, it's Henry! Just before you go can I have a word? ...

Thanks for buying my book; I hope you enjoyed reading it. I am certainly glad that this labour of love is finally out in the open air. It has taken an unbelievable seventeen years to see the light. If you have any constructive comments, questions, or feedback, it would be great to hear from you. The only way I can improve is to act on the advice I receive from my readers. So please help me out.

You can contact me on my Facebook page:
facebook.com/henrybutterfieldauthor
OR
Through my website: www.henry.theauthor.weebly.com
OR
You could always email me at CherrytreePress@gmail.com

Finally, if you get five minutes, could you leave a brief review on Amazon? A couple of lines will be fine. Reviews are the life-blood of authors... and they are read, honest! Just find your way to Amazon.co.uk or if in America, Amazon.co.com and look for "THE COLONEL'S NOTEBOOK" The rest is up to you my friends.

So, to paraphrase what the fat lady (Janet Webb) said at the end of the Morecombe and Wise show each week... "I'd like to thank you for reading my little book. If you've enjoyed it, then it's all been worthwhile. So, until we meet again, cheerio, and I love you all!"
blows kisses

Printed in Great Britain
by Amazon